6/03

$ 10.00

The American History Series

SERIES EDITORS

John Hope Franklin, *Duke University*
A. S. Eisenstadt, *Brooklyn College*

A gift to:

Mynderse Academy Library
2003
in honor of
U.S. History Classes

from

THE MARY BAKER EDDY LIBRARY
FOR THE BETTERMENT OF HUMANITY

Boston, Massachusetts

DISCARD

Allan M. Winkler
Miami University

Home Front U.S.A.

America during World War II

SECOND EDITION

Harlan Davidson, Inc.
Wheeling, Illinois 60090-6000

Library of Congress Cataloging-in-Publication Data

Winkler, Allan M., 1945
      Home front U.S.A.: America during World War II / Alan
      M. Winkler. —2nd ed.
        p. cm.
      Includes bibliographical references (p. 111) and index.

      ISBN 0-88295-983-2 (alk. paper)
      1. United States—History—1933–1945. 2. World War,
1939–1945—United States. I. Title. II. Title: Home front USA
  E806 .W55   2000
  973.917—dc21   99-29896
                                                    CIP

Cover illustration: New York City aluminum collection, 1942.
Courtesy Franklin D. Roosevelt Library

For Henry R. Winkler

FOREWORD

Every generation writes its own history for the reason that it sees the past in the foreshortened perspective of its own experience. This has surely been true of the writing of American history. The practical aim of our historiography is to give us a more informed sense of where we are going by helping us understand the road we took in getting where we are. As the nature and dimensions of American life are changing, so too are the themes of our historical writing. Today's scholars are hard at work reconsidering every major aspect of the nation's past: its politics, diplomacy, economy, society, recreation, mores and values, as well as status, ethnic, race, sexual, and family relations. The lists of series titles that appear on the inside covers of this book will show at once that our historians are ever broadening the range of their studies.

The aim of this series is to offer our readers a survey of what today's historians are saying about the central themes and aspects of the American past. To do this, we have invited to write for the series only scholars who have made notable contributions to the respective fields in which they are working. Drawing on primary and secondary materials, each volume presents a factual and narrative account of its particular subject, one that affords readers a basis for perceiving its larger dimensions and importance. Conscious that readers respond to the closeness and immediacy of a subject, each of our authors seeks to restore the past as an actual

present, to revive it as a living reality. The individuals and groups who figure in the pages of our books appear as real people who once were looking for survival and fulfillment. Aware that historical subjects are often matters of controversy, our authors present their own findings and conclusions. Each volume closes with an extensive critical essay on the writings of the major authorities on its particular theme.

The books in this series are primarily designed for use in both basic and advanced courses in American history, on the undergraduate and graduate levels. Such a series has a particular value these days, when the format of American history courses is being altered to accommodate a greater diversity of reading materials. The series offers a number of distinct advantages. It extends the dimensions of regular course work. It makes clear that the study of our past is, more than the student might otherwise understand, at once complex, profound, and absorbing. It presents that past as a subject of continuing interest and fresh investigation.

For these reasons the series strongly invites an interest that far exceeds the walls of academe. The work of experts in their respective fields, it puts at the disposal of all readers the rich findings of historical inquiry, an invitation to join, in major fields of research, those who are pondering anew the central themes and aspects of our past.

And, going beyond the confines of the classroom, it reminds the general reader no less than the university student that in each successive generation of the ever-changing American adventure, from its very start until our own day, men and women and children were facing their daily problems and attempting, as we are now, to live their lives and to make their way.

John Hope Franklin
A. S. Eisenstadt

ACKNOWLEDGEMENTS

Like its predecessor published in 1986, this second edition of *Home Front U.S.A.* draws both on secondary literature and primary research, but this work also uses a wide range of new accounts that have appeared in the last 15 years.

In writing the first edition, I benefited from the influence of John Morton Blum, my adviser in graduate school, who first introduced me to World War II as he was writing a book about it and encouraged me—and others—to write about it too. I have been interested in the war ever since. Perhaps even more important, he showed me how history could and should be written. At the same time, I appreciated the perceptive criticisms of Richard Polenberg and James T. Patterson, who commented extensively on an early draft of that first edition.

In preparing this edition, as the last one, I am indebted to John W. Jeffries, a fellow student in that first seminar I took with John Blum and a friend ever since. His work has been particularly useful to me in the revision process. I also appreciate continuing conversations with Roger Daniels, a colleague and friend who works nearby, about the war and about the process of writing history in general. Finally, I want to thank my father, Henry R. Winkler, to whom this edition, like the first, is dedicated. He was overseas fighting in World War II when I was born and did not return home until I was a year and a half old. In the years since then, I am grateful for both his professional example and his personal support.

CONTENTS

CHAPTER THREE: **Outsiders and Ethnic Groups** / 54

CHAPTER FOUR: **The Politics of War** / 86

EPILOGUE / 106

PROLOGUE

Participation in World War II had a profound influence on the United States. Although no fighting took place on the American mainland, the war engulfed the nation and became the focus of all its activity between 1942 and 1945. It demanded intense military and diplomatic efforts, at unprecedented levels, to coordinate strategy and tactics with other members of the Grand Alliance. It required a monumental productive effort to provide the materials necessary to fight. And it resulted in a meaningful reorientation of social patterns at home.

The United States became a major force in the war. Although its entrance into the struggle came late—more than two years after hostilities began—America had been increasingly committed to the Allied cause even before the Japanese attack on Pearl Harbor in December 1941 elicited a declaration of war. United States naval convoys had already been protecting shipments of military and economic aid for the beleagured overseas democracies, exports that American factories had been working hard to produce. While the nation's formal entrance into hostilities merely ratified a process already underway, active involvement gave the United States a vested interest in the outcome of the conflict and validated the enormous effort being undertaken by the American people.

In making that ultimately successful effort, American society changed. Ravaged by the Great Depression, the United States re-

mained troubled as that difficult decade came to an end. The war brought a resurgence of optimism after the enormous hardships of the 1930s. Military spending that started in 1940 gave the country's economic system the boost it needed, and the nation began to revive as Americans returned to work to make weapons of war. Outsiders, previously denied access to the American dream, now found themselves with the best jobs they had ever held. Women plunged into war work in ever-increasing numbers and played a major role in home-front production, while African Americans and members of other minority groups demanded and many times received better positions in the industrial sector once it became clear that their participation would make a significant difference in the prosecution of the war.

Between 1940 and 1945, the basic structure of American society became increasingly complex. As the government girded itself for the conflict, bureaucratic organization became even more extensive than it had been during the New Deal. New executive agencies proliferated, and the power of the presidency expanded in response to the demands of war. In virtually every area of home-front activity, Americans confronted shifting social and political issues as they adjusted to new patterns that came to dominate their lives. They embraced changes, even as they clung to old values: Americans wanted a better America *within* the framework of the past.

For the most part, Americans got what they wanted and looked back fondly on the war in subsequent years. They had fought against totalitarian dictatorships for democratic ideals and they had won. The world was a better place for the sacrifices they had made, and veterans as well as those who had peopled the home front took pride in a job well done. For many Americans World War II was, in the phrase journalist Studs Terkel helped popularize in 1984 with the title of his Pulitzer Prize–winning book, *"The Good War."* Yet in the last decade and a half of the twentieth century, that view began to change, at least in the community of scholars seeking to understand the long-term impact of the struggle. Terkel himself placed his title in quotation marks, he noted at the start of his book, "not as a matter of caprice or editorial comment, but simply because the adjective 'good' mated to

the noun 'war' is so incongruous." In the pages that followed, many of the people he interviewed told stories about the horrors they experienced, both on the battlefield and at home, and their reflections made his title, and perceptions about the war itself, all the more ironic.

Scholars began to describe the struggle in much greater complexity than had earlier authors. Literary critic Paul Fussell painted a devastating picture of the struggle in *Wartime: Understanding and Behavior in the Second World War* (1989). "The damage war visited upon bodies and buildings, planes and tanks and ships, is obvious," he wrote. "Less obvious is the damage it did to intellect, discrimination, honesty, individuality, complexity, ambiguity, and irony, not to mention privacy and wit." Richard Polenberg, who authored one of the best early analyses of the home-front experience in 1972, returned to the subject 20 years later in "The Good War? A Reappraisal of How World War II Affected American Society" (*The Virginia Magazine of History and Biography,* 1992). This time he focused less on the positive accomplishments of the struggle and more on the way the war worked "to narrow the scope of individual freedom and to reinforce illiberal tendencies in virtually all areas of life, but especially in class, gender, and race relations."

Other scholars followed suit. In 1993, in *A Democracy at War: America's Fight at Home and Abroad in World War II,* William L. O'Neill observed both "great vitality" and "generosity of spirit" in the conduct of the war but concluded that "America nevertheless failed to live up to its highest principles in very important ways, discriminating against refugees, Japanese-Americans, and blacks, while denying women full equality on the job and in the armed services." These were, he noted, "the liabilities of American democracy . . . that made victory more difficult to achieve than it needed to have been." In 1996, in *Wartime America: The World War II Home Front,* John W. Jeffries drew an even more nuanced portrait of the experience at home. Sorting through "often complicated claims and counterclaims" about the impact of the war, he acknowledged, in the most judicious assessment yet to appear, "both successes and shortcomings."

That debate about the war was reflected more publicly in the mid-1990s in the furious controversy over plans for an exhibit at the Smithsonian Institution in Washington, D.C., to commemorate the fiftieth anniversary of the United States' use of the atomic bomb. The exhibit was intended to feature the *Enola Gay,* the B-29 bomber that dropped the first atomic bomb on Japan on August 6, 1945. Veterans charged that the script and accompanying materials emphasized the bomb's devastation and its postwar environmental consequences without mentioning the carnage suffered in the Pacific War that began with Japan's attack on Pearl Harbor; the exhibit's efforts to present the problematic consequences of atomic weaponry failed to highlight that its use had surely saved *their* lives. When the Smithsonian reworked plans for the display to accommodate the veterans' concerns, historians involved in the project objected that this "historical cleansing" had distorted the entire account. Eventually, when an irritable Congress entered the fray, the Smithsonian canceled its elaborate plans and simply put the fuselage of the *Enola Gay* on display.

While this debate focused on one issue and one exhibit, it was really part of a much larger argument over whose version of the entire war itself should prevail. As Edward T. Linenthal noted in his essay "Anatomy of a Controversy," in a book he co-edited with Tom Engelhardt (*History Wars: The* Enola Gay *and Other Battles for the American Past,* 1996), a "darker narrative" about atomic energy "—particularly when applied to the 'Good War'—seemed to tap into deeper fears about whether or not the United States was a righteous and innocent nation." Was this the noble war, fought for altruistic ends, that the veterans remembered? Or was it a much more complicated struggle that could not be so easily understood?

With each passing year we know more about the triumphs and the tragedies of America's involvement in World War II. Scholarship, particularly in recent years, has deepened our awareness of the accomplishments of both soldiers and civilians and our recognition of the consequences of decisions made. As debates that seemed to intensify at the time of the fiftieth anniversary of the war have begun to fade, we can now examine even more carefully the home-front achievements and repercussions of the greatest struggle of all time.

The Arsenal of Democracy

Mobilization was the first priority as Americans prepared for war. Although the United States had the potential to support the entire Allied effort, resources had to be channeled toward appropriate ends, making enormous organizational adjustments a requirement for the nation to operate on a successful war footing.

It was a daunting task. The economy had been in shambles in the 1930s as the nation struggled with the consequences of the Great Depression. With 25 percent of the workforce unemployed and a similar percentage underemployed, the industrial sector was but a shadow of its past might. As spending for defense in 1940 brought about the economic revival that economist John Maynard Keynes had predicted, the nation discovered the need for centralized direction—to a degree unprecedented in American history—to ensure the timely delivery of essential resources. Slowly, in a series of fits and starts, the United States converted to a war footing and found a way to produce what was needed most.

The President and Mobilization

Presiding over the massive mobilization—and over the entire war effort—was the man who had helped the nation survive the Great Depression. Franklin D. Roosevelt, popularly known as "FDR," played a dominant role in the war. President since 1933, he took the same activist approach he had followed during the New Deal. He engaged in personal diplomacy to help keep the Allies together, made all necessary military decisions, and kept a watchful eye on the domestic side of the struggle. Committed to victory above all else, Roosevelt frequently had to make compromises, particularly on issues that surfaced at home, which occasionally caused him difficulty. Yet FDR retained the ebullient spirit—and infectious grin—that had sustained the nation in the past and would continue to sustain it during the war.

Historians have disagreed about the success of Roosevelt's New Deal in promoting economic recovery and even reform, but most have acknowledged his remarkable charisma. "His personality positively crackled, without as much as a word," observed Kay Summersby, General Dwight D. Eisenhower's wartime chauffeur, the first time she saw FDR. He was—as William E. Leuchtenburg (*Franklin D. Roosevelt and the New Deal, 1932–1940,* 1963 and *In the Shadow of FDR: From Harry Truman to Ronald Reagan,* revised and updated edition, 1989), Arthur M. Schlesinger, Jr. (*The Age of Roosevelt: The Coming of the New Deal,* 1958 and *The Age of Roosevelt: The Politics of Upheaval,* 1960), and James MacGregor Burns (*Roosevelt: The Lion and the Fox,* 1956) all have shown—an extraordinary leader. A member of a wealthy, aristocratic New York family, FDR was nonetheless able to persuade ordinary Americans that he had their interests in mind, and to infuse them with his own boundless optimism and confidence that everything would work out. He struck just the right note in his first inaugural address when he declared, "The only thing we have to fear is fear itself," and he retained public confidence in the days and years that followed.

A master at using the media, Roosevelt made people understand that he cared. Recalling one of FDR's legendary radio-

broadcast "fireside chats," Secretary of Labor Frances Perkins once observed: "His face would smile and light up as though he were actually sitting on the front porch or in the parlor with them. People felt this, and it bound them to him in affection."

Roosevelt was a complex and sometimes mystifying man. "I cannot come to grips with him!" lamented a loyal cabinet member, who spoke for all who worked with FDR. Yet, complaints notwithstanding, affection for the president remained undiminished throughout his tenure. "A second-class intellect,—but a first-class temperament!" Justice Oliver Wendell Holmes once remarked of Roosevelt, and that temperament helped maintain national morale.

Roosevelt fully understood the importance of his role, a role he thoroughly enjoyed playing. He loved visiting the troops in his capacity as commander-in-chief, and he delighted in repeating the response he gave to a soldier in North Africa, who gasped "Oh my god" in astonishment at seeing him. "Just for one more term, son," the president said.

During the war years, Roosevelt governed as he had in the past. "I am a juggler," he once said, according to Doris Kearns Goodwin (*No Ordinary Time: Franklin and Eleanor Roosevelt: The Home Front in World War II,* 1994). "I never let my right hand know what my left hand does." He was fond of creating conflicting layers of authority, as evidenced by his establishment of agencies that competed with others already in existence. That pattern allowed him to play off assistants against one another, thereby giving them the chance to work out their disagreements themselves, or enabling the president to step in to mediate the inevitable disputes himself if he chose.

Roosevelt acted, as always, with a masterful sense of timing. He had the ability to wait, indefinitely if necessary, until the time for action was right. He would agree to see subordinates to discuss matters about which he was undecided, only to ramble on genially for the entire meeting. Marriner Eccles, governor of the Federal Reserve Board, once recalled how an important meeting in the late 1930s never got started, for his allotted time was taken up watching FDR play with his little dog Fala and then scold the pet for "purging himself on the rug." At first furious, Eccles later realized

that he had been a victim of the president's way of avoiding controversial situations until he was ready to act.

During the war, as Goodwin has noted in *No Ordinary Time,* "There were indeed many times, as those who worked with him observed, when it seemed that he could truly see it all—the relation of the home front to the war front; of the factories to the soldiers; of speeches to morale; of the government to the people; of war aims to the shape of the peace to come."

Well aware of the need for massive production, Roosevelt applied his executive talents to the prickly problem of industrial mobilization. As war in Europe threatened in the late 1930s, American industry remained sluggish, still caught in the cycle of the depression. When the war broke out in September 1939, and the Axis powers—Germany and Italy—quickly established their dominance on the European continent, the president began to worry in earnest, for he recognized how important American production would be to the war effort. In May 1940, he asked Congress to appropriate $1 billion for the production of 50,000 planes. He soon requested even more money. Well before the Japanese attack on Pearl Harbor, Roosevelt declared, "We must be the great arsenal of democracy."

Although Roosevelt insisted on "speed and speed now," it took time for the economy to gear up, as the country's difficulties were immense. John Morton Blum was one of the first scholars to examine the thorny problems that had to be overcome, in *From the Morgenthau Diaries: Years of War, 1941–1945* (1967). Not until mid-1943 was a rational system of economic controls firmly in place. Conversion to a military footing was a complicated process that required central direction, but that direction arrived only after months, even years, of experimentation. As was so often the case, Roosevelt tried first one agency, then another, until he finally found a combination that worked.

Roosevelt's first attempt at direction came in 1939, when he appointed a War Resources Board to examine the needs involved in regulation of the economy. Concerned about antiwar sentiment, however, and wary of excessive planning, FDR withheld his own support. "I do not believe that there is an awful lot of

Government action that is needed at the present time," he declared in May 1940.

The German blitzkrieg of the Low Countries and France that year changed his mind. To provide better coordination, Roosevelt resurrected the National Defense Advisory Commission, which had functioned during World War I. Its members represented industry, labor, agriculture, and the consuming public, and the agency had several divisions, each concerned with a different aspect of war mobilization. But the commission proved singularly ineffective, for it had only advisory authority and lacked a responsible head.

Also, before America entered the war, Roosevelt created the Office of Production Management (in January 1941). He intended this agency to stimulate industrial production and resolve manpower and raw materials problems. Codirected by William Knudsen of General Motors and Sidney Hillman of the Amalgamated Clothing Workers of America, it tried to encourage manufacturers to place military needs over civilian desires, but the agency lacked the statutory authority to back up its requests, ran into trouble stemming from divided leadership, and eventually broke down— as soon as military requirements for scarce materials outstripped supply.

The failure of the Office of Production Management led to the creation of the War Production Board (WPB) in January 1942. Roosevelt chose Donald Nelson, who had enjoyed a successful business career with Sears, Roebuck & Co., to head the new agency, and gave it the mandate to "exercise general responsibility" over the economy. With the government now requiring civilian industries to convert to military production, the WPB sought to curtail nonessential civilian activity and to implement a system of preferences and priorities.

The WPB soon suffered from its decision to allow the army and navy to retain responsibility for military procurement. With the armed services intruding on its organizational efforts, the WPB lost the ability to impose central direction, at a time when the economy faced keen demands from all sectors. As the system threatened to break down, the WPB implemented a new Con-

trolled Materials Plan aimed at coordinating needs and supplies, but this did little to help the agency craft a central economic direction. As Bruce Catton argued passionately in *The Warlords of Washington* (1948), which provided scholars with an interpretive focus in subsequent years, military and business interests simply took precedence over all other concerns.

Nelson was confronted with additional problems when he acquiesced in Roosevelt's decision to appoint "czars" to deal with the problematic shortages of manpower, petroleum, and rubber. Bernard Baruch, who had been responsible for industrial coordination during World War I, warned him that "you must be the boss and when you say anything . . . it just has to go." Yet Nelson found himself unable to act decisively. As one of his associates later observed, "One of these War Department Generals will stick a knife into Nelson and all Nelson does is pull the knife out and hand it back and say, 'General, I believe you dropped something.' And the general will say, 'Why Don, thanks, I believe I did'—and right away he sticks it back in again."

Roosevelt acted once again in May 1943. When military leaders proved unwilling to work with Nelson any longer, the president created another new agency, the Office of War Mobilization (OWM), to be led by James F. Byrnes. Byrnes, formerly a member of the Supreme Court after service as a senator from South Carolina, had most recently headed the Office of Economic Stabilization, where he mediated disputes between various wartime agencies. The OWM, superimposed on existing organizations, was given policymaking authority and became a court of final appeal when industrial arguments occurred. Byrnes assumed neither operating functions nor administrative chores. Rather, he successfully used his political savvy to provide needed coordination. Byrnes's job was summed up by a WPB official: "Suppose you and I have a disagreement in arithmetic; you claim that two and two make four, while I claim that two and two makes six. We take it to Jimmy Byrnes for a decision. He's apt to get us both to agree that two and two make five." With Byrnes in charge of the OWM, FDR had finally achieved the coordination he needed.

Industrial Mobilization

Conversion to a war economy was not easy. Ever mindful of the need for speed, the government encountered problems in every area. A case in point was the experience with the automobile industry, which was crucial to industrial mobilization. Its assembly lines were needed to make planes and tanks, and it was asked to produce one-fifth of all war material in the United States. But car manufacturers were in no hurry. With the country recovering from the depression, their priority was the huge civilian market coupled with Americans' renewed purchasing power, which translated into large profits. In 1941, they produced nearly 1 million more cars than they had in 1939. The WPB, at its first meeting, had to outlaw production of cars and trucks so that manufacture of military vehicles could begin. Even then extensions and exemptions complicated the process until the spring of 1942.

Once conversion finally began there was no stopping it. In the summer of 1940, Packard accepted a contract for 9,000 Rolls Royce engines, and Chrysler agreed to produce tanks in a plant scheduled to be built north of Detroit. An even more dramatic venture was the bomber plant built by Henry Ford in southeastern Michigan. When Ford agreed, near the end of 1940, to construct 1,200 B-24 bombers, he planned a gigantic new factory, to be erected 35 miles from Detroit in an area called Willow Run. The mile-long plant, with the main building alone covering 67 acres, was to assemble the airplanes on a single, continuous assembly line. Groundbreaking on the Willow Run facility occurred in April 1941; the first parts were produced late that year; the first bomber appeared the following year. At a final cost of $65 million, the plant contained over 1,600 pieces of heavy machinery as well as 7,500 jigs and other fixtures. When working at full tilt, it employed over 42,000 people. It was, aviator Charles Lindbergh observed, "a sort of Grand Canyon of the mechanized world."

Other ventures were similarly successful. Early in the war the United States found itself facing a serious rubber shortage, as William M. Tuttle, Jr., has noted in "The Birth of an Industry: The Synthetic

Rubber 'Mess' in World War II" (*Technology and Culture,* 1981). Japan's seizure of the Dutch East Indies and Malaya had cut off more than 90 percent of America's crude rubber supply, and the half a million tons stockpiled would only meet demand for one year. Production of synthetic rubber would have been the easy answer, but the process in the United States had been slowed down in the late 1920s by an agreement between Standard Oil of New Jersey and I. G. Farbenindustrie, the German chemical firm, that squelched American efforts in the area. That agreement may have helped American business at the time, yet it clearly hampered the public interest now.

But with the war underway and the cartel agreement no longer binding, Americans began to consider the creation of synthetic rubber anew, and two different substances—grain alcohol and petroleum—were key ingredients in two possible processes. Not surprisingly, agricultural interests pushed a bill through Congress in the summer of 1942 that would have favored the alcohol method, and petroleum administrator Harold Ickes endorsed the petroleum approach. In the end FDR vetoed the bill. As the nation embarked upon rubber drives and rationing programs, production of synthetic rubber using both processes began. The president appointed William Jeffers rubber director in late 1942, and the government spent $700 million to build 51 plants that rubber companies then leased. One West Virginia factory run by the United States Rubber Company covered 77 acres and produced 90,000 tons a year. The program was a success, and capacity increased steadily. By 1944, the nation was producing more than 800,000 tons of rubber a year, approximately 87 percent of the total amount used. Another major problem had been overcome.

The American effort to create an atomic bomb was one more area in which American productive strength made a difference. For several decades after the war, historians studying the bomb concentrated on the decision to use atomic weapons in 1945. The process of developing the bomb, however, was crucial to the question of its ultimate use. With the declassification of relevant documents, Martin J. Sherwin (*A World Destroyed: The Atomic Bomb and the Grand Alliance, 1941–1945,* 1975), Barton J. Bernstein

("Roosevelt, Truman, and the Atomic Bomb, 1941–1945: A Reinterpretation" *Political Science Quarterly*, 1975), and others have shown vividly what happened in the years before 1945. In August 1939, physicist Albert Einstein wrote Roosevelt a letter in which he observed that "it is conceivable . . . that extremely powerful bombs of a new type may . . . be constructed," and he hinted that the Germans were interested in the possibility. Roosevelt established a committee to look into the matter, but there was little sense of urgency until actual American involvement in the war. After several bureaucratic reorganizations, and a stronger executive commitment, the task of creating an atomic bomb began. It was known as the Manhattan Project.

The United States devoted a great deal of effort to this top-secret quest, described by Richard Rhodes (*The Making of the Atomic Bomb,* 1986) and Allan M. Winkler (*Life Under a Cloud: American Anxiety about the Atom,* 1993). The project included the construction and use of 37 installations in the United States and Canada. New cities were erected at Oak Ridge, Tennessee, at Hanford, Washington, and at Los Alamos, New Mexico. The Manhattan Project, which cost $2 billion—at the time a huge sum of money—employed 120,000 people. It also created a scientific infrastructure, largely supported by the government, that continued after the war. After producing the first self-sustaining atomic chain reaction in history, American scientists then had to find a way to gather enough of a special form of uranium, or produce enough plutonium, to construct a working bomb.

In July 1945, three months after Roosevelt died, the monumental program paid off. At Alamogordo, in the New Mexico desert, scientists finally tested the first atomic device. It was a stunning success: the explosion broke windows 125 miles away and unleashed so much energy that a blind woman saw light. Now the United States grappled with the question of how, and whether, to use its immensely powerful new weapon. Although there were other alternatives, as J. Samuel Walker has shown in *Prompt and Utter Destruction: Truman and the Use of Atomic Bombs against Japan* (1997), it was "an easy and obvious military decision." The bomb had always been intended for military use, and planners continued

to operate on the basis of that assumption. In August, the first two atomic weapons were dropped on Hiroshima and Nagasaki in Japan, killing tens of thousands of Japanese civilians, in an ultimately successful effort to end the war.

Other government-directed scientific projects likewise played an important role in the conflict. The British invention of a new radar transmitter called a cavity magnetron led to an intensive effort, centered at the Massachusetts Institute of Technology, to determine the best military application of the new device. The Radiation Laboratory at MIT, ten of whose members later won the Nobel Prize, designed innovative radar systems that helped the Allies track German submarines and drop bombs more accurately in both the European and Pacific theaters of war.

Mobilization and the Business Community

Mobilization on all fronts worked because business interests were squarely behind the effort. Businessmen had fallen on hard times during the Great Depression, and had found their reputations tarnished. Roosevelt himself had lashed out at them during the 1930s, when he perceived they were resisting governmental programs aimed at promoting recovery. Businessmen, he once said, "are unanimous in their hatred for me—and I welcome their hatred." Though FDR never intended to dismantle the capitalist system, he could, in the country's worst economic crisis, afford angry, anticapitalist rhetoric when it suited his ends. Now, however, he needed business's help.

Secretary of War Henry L. Stimson, a Republican in a Democratic administration, understood exactly what was necessary to meet production requirements. "If you are going to try to go to war, or to prepare for war, in a capitalist country," he said, "you have got to let business make money out of the process or business won't work." The government therefore chose to work on big business's terms, providing incentives and tax breaks that effectively underwrote the expense of plant expansion. Corporations manufacturing essential goods were permitted to depreciate the cost of conversion over a five-year period in a way that cut back on

taxable income. Furthermore, firms could recover excess-profits taxes paid during the war if they could show a postwar loss. One economist later termed the arrangement "the biggest and most resilient cushion in the history of public finance." The government also granted firms immunity from antitrust prosecution if they could show that cooperative arrangements would enhance essential war production.

An even more important incentive for business was the cost-plus-a-fixed-fee system, whereby the government guaranteed all development and production costs and then paid a percentage profit on the wartime goods produced. With frequent design changes demanded and improvements required, business was understandably reluctant to spend large sums of money that were hard to estimate in advance. As the government suspended competitive bidding and simply urged chosen firms to do whatever was necessary without regard to cost, business found it could not lose, for the government assumed all the risks. Though this approach caused a measure of waste, the urgency of military demands allowed the process to continue.

Novelist Hariette Arnow vividly characterized the cost-plus system in her powerful novel *The Dollmaker* (1954). According to one of its characters:

These big men that owns these factories, th' gover'mint gives em profits on what things cost—six cents on th' dollar I've heard say. So every time they can make a thing cost two dollars stid a one . . . they're six cents ahead, an everybody's happy. Th' more men, th' more plus fer th' owners, th' more money an more men fer them unions, I figger.

Businessmen used their ingenuity to make the most of their unique opportunities. Henry Ford's Willow Run plant gained favorable publicity for its use of midgets within small fuselage and wing spaces. But other entrepreneurs, as John Morton Blum has revealed in *V Was for Victory: Politics and American Culture During World War II* (1976), were even more successful in using war demands for economic gain.

Robert Woodruff, head of Coca-Cola, was a case in point. He persuaded the army and navy that Coke was an essential drink,

one well suited to the needs of soldiers and sailors. Despite sugar shortages at home, he was able to get what he needed and to transport syrup, bottles, and, eventually, entire production facilities overseas wherever American troops were deployed. In this way, Woodruff developed a universal taste for Coca-Cola, and it became and remained the most extensively distributed mass-produced product in the world.

Philip K. Wrigley, the chewing gum magnate, was equally successful in identifying his product as an essential war good. He supplied a stick of gum for each K ration package used to feed military personnel, and he even agreed to pack the containers in his own plants. At the same time, he sought to market gum to civilians by playing on his military connection. His advertisements stressed that gum could help war workers, just like soldiers, relax in periods of stress. "To help your workers feel better—work better," he said, "just see that they get five sticks of chewing gum every day."

Then there was Henry J. Kaiser, the shipbuilder who became something of a hero for his ability to get things done. Previously the head of one arm of a consortium—the Six Companies—that had built the Boulder, Bonneville, and Grand Coulee dams, he now turned his attention to ships. Using his contacts and connections as well as huge amounts of government capital, as Stephen B. Adams (*Mr. Kaiser Goes to Washington: The Rise of a Government Entrepreneur,* 1997) has shown, Kaiser produced tankers, troop ships, landing ships, and destroyer escorts—and was responsible for constructing 30 percent of all the ships built in 1943. He became best known for his Liberty ships—merchant vessels made by mass-production methods—which became the major wartime cargo carriers. Prefabrication was the key to his success. In 1941, construction time was 355 days. Kaiser cut that down to 56 days the next year and, in a remarkable demonstration of speed, even turned out a vessel in 14 days. Though one ship broke apart dramatically on the pier before sailing, Kaiser's reputation remained untainted.

All sorts of businessmen with expertise to contribute streamed into Washington, D.C., to work in the agencies and commissions

responsible for coordinating the production process at the national level. "Dollar-a-year" men, who were permitted to stay on their company payrolls to preclude their sacrificing regular incomes while working for the federal government, arrived by the thousands. Eventually, these men made up three-fourths of the executive staff of the WPB.

In the cabinet, Henry Stimson and Secretary of the Navy Frank Knox staffed their departments with men from the major corporate law firms and investment banking houses of Boston and New York. John Lord O'Brien, Robert Lovett, John J. McCloy, Robert Patterson, and James Forrestal were among those who assumed positions of prominence in the wartime government. All of these men kept national interests in mind as they worked on behalf of the war effort, but they also brought with them different assumptions about the nature and role of government than those held by New Dealers in the 1930s. They believed in big business, in its ability to get things done, and in its need to be relatively unhampered by centralized restrictions. Their values had been challenged during the depression years, but with huge national production requirements to be met, those values now regained ascendancy. Business leaders found they had a relatively free hand to use their own channels and connections to help win the war.

Inevitably, governmental priorities changed. Under the influence of business interests, there was a good deal of centralization and concentration. Contracts went to the largest firms, whose operating officers often knew officials in Washington. There were obvious advantages to relying on the nation's major companies, for they already had the labor pools and assembly lines that could most easily be converted to war production. They also already had research staffs that could be quickly mobilized to make the necessary refinements in war items. The large firms subcontracted tasks to smaller companies, but even so, many of the nation's smaller firms, blocked from supplies of scarce materials and unable to produce civilian goods, had to close their doors.

Statistics tell part of the story. *Business Week* declared that after two months of war there were 200,000 fewer employers in the nation. It was, the magazine said, the "most severe contraction in

the business population that we have ever experienced." According to United States Department of Commerce estimates, 300,000 retailers shut down in 1942. Altogether, over half a million small businesses failed during the war.

Meanwhile, the large firms got larger. In 1940, as the defense program began, 175,000 companies accounted for 70 percent of the nation's manufacturing output, while 100 other companies provided the remaining 30 percent. By March 1943, with twice as much being produced, the ratio was reversed: now the 100 companies that had produced 30 percent in 1940 held contracts for 70 percent of all defense production.

Congress mandated the creation of a Smaller War Plants Corporation in mid-1942, but it never worked successfully. The corporation's creation was an attempt to legislate a vision of society in which the small entrepreneur had a chance, but that vision gave way in the face of the demand for rapid production to assist in the conduct of the war. Though small businesses hoped for a revival in the postwar period, the creation of an early version of the "military-industrial complex" during the struggle provided a framework that favored the industrial giants, in wartime and in the ensuing years.

Liberals who hoped that the war would provide a model for centralization and direction of the economy in peacetime were disappointed. As Alan Brinkley has shown in *The End of Reform: New Deal Liberalism in Recession and War* (1995), the experience of mobilization "served not as a model to liberals, but as a warning." Micromanaging an economy as complex as that of the United States might work in the short term, but could not be sustained over a longer period of time. Future direction of the economy would have to come by use of the fiscal tools of spending and taxation.

Mobilization and the Workforce

Though business interests played a major role in mobilizing the productive might of America during the war, business was not the only sector involved in the process. Without the cooperation of the

nation's workforce, the United States could never have accomplished the economic miracles that resulted in victory for the Allies.

Workers welcomed the conversion to a war footing, for it heralded an end to the ubiquitous unemployment of the 1930s. Once the United States began to organize for defense in 1940, jobs became more readily available. Employment opportunities were even greater after the nation entered the war in late 1941.

The workforce expanded astronomically to meet production demands. Three times as many men and women joined the military as in World War I, while others quickly took the newly vacated civilian positions. More than 15 million people entered either the armed services or the labor force between 1940 and 1943. By the latter year, the unemployment rate stood at 1.3 percent, less than one-tenth of the figure in 1937, the *best* year during the Great Depression. Between 1939 and 1945, the number of jobless people dropped from 9 million to 1 million, with jobs available to virtually anyone who wanted to work.

One problem that had to be addressed was how to channel workers to jobs in which they could be most useful to the war effort. Coordination was necessary in the labor sector, just as it was in the business sector. In the spring of 1942, Roosevelt created a War Manpower Commission (WMC) headed by Paul V. McNutt, former governor of Indiana. Its purpose was to try to determine how workers could best be used, but it lacked power to require adherence to its directives. At the end of the year, seeking to enhance the commission's authority, the president transferred the selective service to the WMC. Efforts to render work assignments compulsory as a way of making the best use of the labor pool, however, ran into political opposition. Only by the fall of 1943 did the administration come up with a more flexible manpower plan that provided a mechanism for making sure workers were available where needed.

The increased workforce buttressed the growing union movement. Labor had come of age with the governmental support of the New Deal in the 1930s. Section 7a of the National Industrial Recovery Act in 1933 had affirmed labor's right to organize, and the National Labor Relations Act—the Wagner Act—in 1935 had pro-

vided the mechanism for union recognition and collective bargaining. During these years, the American Federation of Labor (AFL) added millions of workers to its ranks, while the Congress of Industrial Organizations (CIO) undertook to organize basic industry in the United States.

Despite labor's internal splits, the war enhanced unionization. In 1935, the AFL had expelled more aggressive CIO leaders from the organization, prompting the fledgling CIO to go its own way. As assembly-line production made craft distinctions less meaningful, more and more jurisdictional disputes took place. In spite of labor unions' overarching common interests, a serious rivalry between the two umbrella organizations remained. "We will fight against a movement which has vowed to destroy us and wipe us off the face of the earth," AFL leader William Green declared in late 1941, referring to the CIO.

Yet unions of all sorts continued to grow. In the defense period just prior to Pearl Harbor, union membership increased by 1.5 million, and unions scored a number of impressive gains. In 1941, for example, the United Automobile Workers received a contract from Ford stipulating a "union shop"—a place where workers must be members of a labor organization—and a dues checkoff—monies automatically deducted from an employee's paycheck.

Union growth likewise increased during the war itself. Union membership rose from 10.5 million in 1941 to 14.75 million in 1945. The portion of the workforce enrolled in collective bargaining agreements rose from 30 percent to 45 percent. The CIO made the greatest gains. It became established in the major mass-production industries—steel, rubber, and automobiles—and was almost the size of the older AFL by the end of the war.

Unions benefited from new policies. One of these was a "maintenance-of-membership" formula established by the National War Labor Board (NWLB), which had been created in early 1942 to address labor conflicts during the war. Employers, now bolstered by a large labor pool, argued that a union shop deprived workers of the freedom *not* to choose unionization. The NWLB's formula, aimed at securing labor's cooperation, specified that a union member who failed to quit a union within fifteen days of

signing an employment contract would remain a member of that union for the duration of the contract. This policy preserved a measure of free choice for the worker while protecting union membership levels.

Most historians studying labor trends have acknowledged that industrial union activity came of age during the war. Labor and management, committed to a common goal, learned to talk together and, under government direction, bargain collectively. The whole process enhanced industrial stability and provided workers with more job security than they had ever known. At the same time, as Nelson Lichtenstein has shown in *Labor's War at Home: The CIO in World War II* (1982), wartime pressures weakened the independence and radical drive of the industrial union movement and promoted instead routinized forms of bureaucratic activity, rendering unionism much less militant than it had been in the 1930s. Unions, according to Alan Brinkley (*The End of Reform*), ceased pushing for structural economic reform or the redistribution of wealth and power and focused instead on economic growth through increased consumption in a pattern that continued in the postwar years.

Without question, union members prospered throughout the war. The results were visible in clear economic terms, as workers' wages rose steadily. Average weekly earnings for people involved in manufacturing increased 65 percent—from $32.18 to $47.12 in the 40 months after December 1941. Even after corrections for inflation, real earnings rose 27 percent in manufacturing work. Though there were caps on the increases that were possible in wage rates, total paychecks swelled as employees worked longer hours. The average workweek expanded from 40.6 hours to 45.2 hours between 1941 and 1942; in some factories the norm became a 50- or 60-hour workweek. And virtually all workers put in some overtime for which they were paid time-and-a-half.

Though they complained about the growing differential between their wage rates and business profits, workers plunged in and did what was necessary to produce the implements of war. Don Johnson, an employee of the AC Spark Plug Division of General Motors in Flint, Michigan, observed later that:

After Pearl Harbor there was an immediate change in people's attitude toward their work—their sense of urgency, their dedication, their team work. When the chips were down, people dealt with it like survival. Things that might have taken days longer were done to meet a target so you didn't hold somebody else up—even if it meant putting in extra hours and extra effort.

Johnson went on to describe how right after American entrance into the war, he and others were assigned the task of producing a new item—a navigational computer bomb sight. Though the parent company had doubts about whether the division could do it, the workers did not: "There was never any doubt on our part that we would do what we'd committed ourselves to do. We just did not accept 'Can't do.'"

Farmers too played an important part in the mobilization process. The overall farm population declined by nearly 20 percent during the war, as more than 6 million Americans left their land to join the armed forces or work in urban factories. Clovis Nevels, one of the protagonists in *The Dollmaker*, reflected this migration away from the farm as he left Kentucky to work in the factories of Detroit. Like many tenant farmers in reality, he hoped to find new opportunities in the big city.

But those who stayed behind prospered. According to Walter W. Wilcox (*The Farmer in the Second World War,* 1947), they managed to put the specter of depression behind them. After following the federal policy of crop restriction (the government's effort to impose price stability) during the 1930s, farmers now found themselves encouraged to produce all they could—and more. To meet the unprecedented demand they extended the use of commercial fertilizer and embarked on other soil and crop improvements that increased yields during the war years. As they added to their stores of mechanical equipment—tractors, trucks, grain combines—they were able to expand crop acreage. Using scientific knowledge and technological advances, farmers rose to the challenge and met the wartime demands for more food.

They also secured government support for high farm prices. Through the Farm Bureau Federation, a lobbying organization, and the farm bloc in Congress, they successfully pressed for stan-

dards that benefited them. Farmers had prospered between 1910 and 1914, and the ratio between agricultural and industrial prices in those years had come to be defined as "parity." In early 1942, Congress acceded to farmers' pressure in return for votes needed to establish other controls, setting farm price ceilings at 110 percent of parity. During the war, farm prices more than doubled.

With that congressional assistance, and costs checked by other controls, farmers' profits soared. Net farm income increased from $5.3 billion in 1939 to $13.6 billion in 1944. During the war years, per-capita farm income tripled, while per-capita industrial income only doubled.

Farmers finally had a chance to improve their material circumstances. They could reduce indebtedness, leave positions of tenancy, and build new structures only imagined before. Laura Briggs, a member of a farm family from Idaho, noted that "as farm prices got better and better, the farmers suddenly became the wealth of the community. . . . Farm times became good times. Dad started having his land improved, and of course we improved our home and the outbuildings. We and most other farmers went from a tar-paper shack to a new frame house with indoor plumbing."

World War II brought the farmers a new prosperity; they contributed their resources to the process of mobilization and production, and they benefited from the results. Like members of other groups, they managed to extricate themselves from the troubling cycles of the Great Depression and to enjoy better times after years of poverty and despair. For the farmers, the war marked a time that agricultural historians have come to call the "second American agricultural revolution."

Mobilization and Money

Mobilization in all areas succeeded because government was willing to spend whatever was necessary to win the war. Expenditure levels rose to new heights. Total federal outlays increased from $8.9 billion in 1939 to $98.4 billion in 1945, and simultaneously the gross national product rose from $90.5 billion to $211.9 billion. "Where's the money coming from?" economist Stuart Chase

asked in 1942. "Nobody gives a damn. That is just the point. In the old economy, such reckless outlays would have spelled bankruptcy and ruin. Money came first and men came second. In the new economy, no nation will permit bankruptcy and ruin so long as men, materials, and energy are available. Men first, money second."

In fact, the money came from a number of different sources. The war was financed by both taxation and borrowing. Taxes, which had defrayed 30 percent of the cost of World War I, accounted for almost 50 percent of the cost of World War II. Roosevelt would have preferred to use taxes to cover the entire cost, noting at the end of 1942, "I would rather pay one hundred percent of taxes now than push the burden of this war onto the shoulders of my grandchildren." But the tax structure was inadequate, and the United States was obliged to borrow the rest of what it needed. That money came from both banks and private investors. The sale of war bonds was one important source of income. The U.S. Treasury Department raised $12.9 billion in the first war loan drive in late 1942, $135 billion in the entire series of drives.

Wartime spending energized the economy. Economic historians such as Robert Lekachman (*The Age of Keynes,* 1966) have shown how such spending brought the return of prosperity to the United States. The enormous mobilization effort proved to be the stimulus the country had been lacking for so long. Deliberate, sustained, countercyclical spending brought just the improvement that English economist John Maynard Keynes had predicted.

Keynes had published his major work, *The General Theory of Employment, Interest and Money,* in 1936, but even earlier he had lectured about the same ideas found in this book to his Cambridge University students. He argued that depression was more than a single phase in the business cycle that would inevitably rebound. Rather, Keynes claimed, depression was equilibrium at a very low level that would persist unless enough spending occurred to revive the stalled system. The needed funds might derive from the private sector, through traditional forms of investment, or from the public sector, through aggressive government spending programs or sizable tax cuts. Anything that increased the amount of money in circulation could work.

Keynes had met briefly with Roosevelt in 1934, but the two men had misunderstood one another. "He left a whole rigmarole of figures," the president had commented of Keynes. "He must be a mathematician rather than a political scientist." Keynes in turn had "supposed the President was more literate, economically speaking." For all of the activity during the New Deal, Keynesian theory was never really tried; the nation never committed itself to the deficit spending that might have ended the depression. Conflicting priorities compromised a commitment to recovery alone. The various government initiatives of the 1930s worked in conflicting and contradictory ways, bringing relief to those hardest hit and reform to the system, but failing to generate the needed economic revival.

Then, in 1940, the massive spending that Keynes had called for began to occur. When the United States started to mobilize for defense, the economy improved overnight. "Retail sales began to jump, factories began howling for men, unemployment figures tumbled downhill," Stuart Chase noted. "The backbone of the depression was broken." That improvement gave cause for optimism about the future. "We have seen the last of our great depressions," wartime administrator Chester Bowles declared, "for the simple reason that the public [is] wise enough to know it doesn't have to stand for one."

The results as the economy moved into full gear were stupendous. The huge goals for 1942—60,000 planes, 45,000 tanks, 20,000 antiaircraft guns, and 8 million tons of merchant shipping—were raised still higher for the next year; now the president called for 125,000 planes, 75,000 tanks, 35,000 antiaircraft guns, and 10 million tons of merchant shipping. The industrial system responded by producing what was needed.

Productivity rose dramatically. By 1944, there were 12.5 percent more people in the workforce producing 57 percent more goods. In the manufacturing sector, productivity increased 25 percent between 1939 and 1944, compared to an average yearly rise of 1.9 percent in the period between 1889 and 1939. According to the Department of Commerce, output per worker was one-third greater in 1943 than it had been in 1939.

The index of industrial production reflected the gains. Equal to 100 in the period from 1935 to 1939, it rose to 239 during the war years. In the durable manufactured goods sector, it reached 360.

In every area the figures told the same story. By the middle of 1945, the United States had produced 80,000 landing craft, 100,000 tanks and armored cars, 300,000 airplanes, 15 million guns, and 41 billion rounds of ammunition. Production consumed 434 million tons of steel. It also resulted in two atomic bombs.

Never before had American industry operated at full tilt. But as the conflict raged there was no concern about overproduction. Output alone, to the degree possible, was all that mattered as the United States attempted to make whatever materials were necessary to defeat the Axis powers.

Industrial success was matched by agricultural achievement as well. Livestock output increased 23 percent, crop output by 14 percent. Between 1940 and 1945, there was a 36 percent increase in productivity as the number of persons supplied per farm worker rose from 10.7 to 14.6. Farmers who had worried about raising too much in the past now found themselves called on to produce all they could, a call to which they responded enthusiastically.

America's extraordinary productive capacity, and its ability to harness and develop that capacity relatively quickly, made the crucial difference in the war. A year after Pearl Harbor, the nation was producing more than all its enemies combined. At the Teheran Conference in 1943, Soviet leader Joseph Stalin's toast singled out the accomplishments of the United States: "To American production, without which this war would have been lost."

Conclusion

Mobilization had not been easy, but it had been accomplished. Hesitation had been overcome as the difficult process of conversion had taken place. As enormous changes occurred, the industrial system became more regimented than it had ever been. The federal government provided the centralized direction it had only partially managed to muster in World War I. Agency followed agency, as FDR tried first one expedient, then another, until he

found a system of coordination that worked. The bureaucratic lines were often blurred, as was so often the case during Roosevelt's tenure. But despite the occasional administrative redundancy, the system worked. Scarce materials found their way to the plants where they were needed most and were crafted into the products required to fight.

With the proper incentives, business did what was necessary on all fronts, and business leaders enjoyed revived prominence and prestige. Even as they occasionally grumbled about controls, they took advantage of the system they helped craft to earn the profits they had missed in the 1930s. Workers were delighted to be employed once more, often in positions more responsible or challenging than prior ones. They too grumbled about limitations and constraints, and they sought higher wages than either business or government was willing to grant. But, as they enjoyed the ancillary benefits of the struggle, they had to acknowledge that they were better off than they had been in the past.

And so the United States mobilized for war, with mobilization providing the framework within which all home-front activity unfolded. It brought the revival of prosperity, raising spirits that had flagged during the Great Depression. It generated new opportunities for assorted segments of the workforce and thereby created expectations for the postwar years. It also conditioned the political climate as new officials gained prominence and new issues emerged. Mobilization was a major part of the home-front experience: it changed American society as much as it decided the outcome of the war.

American Society at War

The United States was more fortunate than most other nations involved in World War II. American soldiers fought overseas, and virtually every family had someone in uniform—but after Pearl Harbor no fighting took place on American shores. For the most part, the home-front population was far more comfortable than it had been in the preceding decade. Mobilization brought the return of prosperity, and with it the hope and confidence in the American way that had all but disappeared during the Great Depression. Within the United States, the wartime mood was buoyant and upbeat.

Americans participated in the war in countless ways. Combat soldiers put their lives on the line, in both the European and Pacific theaters of war, and many of these people made the ultimate sacrifice. Civilians at home found themselves engaged in the conflict in other ways. Wartime employees worked hard to accomplish the necessary miracles of production and now had money in their pockets to enjoy what they could once again afford to buy. The government encouraged their involvement in drives and campaigns both to fund the war and to collect necessary resources, and to give them a sense of identification with a common cause.

Some Americans faced problems, to be sure. Migration to cities where there was war work brought discomfort and dislocation both to new arrivals and older residents. Employees, while grateful for their paychecks, still complained—and struck—when wages fell behind profits as owners and industrialists got rich. Workers in new war plants often found housing conditions uncomfortable at best since home building seldom kept pace with population growth. Still, on balance, Americans at home prospered during the war and enjoyed the experience.

Mood and Morale

Americans had a sense of shared purpose once they entered the war. Oral histories have added an important dimension to the study of the struggle by showing how ordinary Americans reacted and responded. First-person accounts, particularly those by Studs Terkel ("*The Good War*") and Mark Jonathon Harris, Franklin D. Mitchell, and Steven J. Schechter (*The Homefront: America during World War II*, 1984), have underscored the feeling of commitment. The Japanese attack on Pearl Harbor on December 7, 1941, brought a sense of unity to the United States. The nation had been divided in the late 1930s as the rest of the world moved toward war. Isolationists in America shunned involvement in the larger struggle and resisted the administration's progressive actions to provide the materials antifascist nations needed for their defense, claiming that the United States was committing itself inevitably to war.

The Pearl Harbor attack—which came without warning—jolted the nation. It destroyed or disabled 19 ships, including 5 battleships, and 150 planes, and left nearly 2,400 servicemen dead. Initially, Americans felt sheer shock; then shock turned to rage. Millions never forgot where they were or what they were doing when they heard the news. Don Johnson, from Flint, Michigan, echoed the sentiments many held as he recalled his reactions after learning of the catastrophe: "First it was indignation, then it turned to anger, and by the time one went to work the following morning it was determination: 'They can't do that to us.'"

Some people were afraid. The number of damaged ships increased as the story of the attack was repeated, and rumors spread

about the next strike. Dennis Keegan, a student at the University of San Francisco, came home to find his landlady screaming, "Dennis, turn the lights out! The Japs are comin'! The Japs are comin'! The Golden Gate Bridge has been bombed."

Americans recognized almost instinctively that Pearl Harbor marked a turning point in their lives. After the attack, nothing would ever be the same. War meant adjustments to new patterns and disruptions to be overcome, and forced a rapid growing up. Jean Bartlett, a fourteen year old from Berkeley, California, later recalled: "On December 6, 1941, I was playing with paper dolls: Deanna Durbin, Sonja Henie. I had a Shirley Temple doll that I cherished. After Pearl Harbor, I never played with dolls again."

Franklin Roosevelt gave focus to Americans' feelings as he addressed Congress the next day. Calling December 7 "a date which will live in infamy," he asked Congress to declare "that since the unprovoked and dastardly attack . . . a state of war has existed." Sixty million Americans listening to their radios heard the president's speech. They understood that long-smoldering tensions had led to an unavoidable war.

At the same time, with the period of waiting finally over, they felt relieved. Now the nation could commit itself more fully to the task at hand. Secretary of War Stimson summed up the prevailing sentiments of most of those in the government when he said, "My first feeling was of relief that the indecision was over and that a crisis had come in a way which would unite all our people." The attack created a sense of common danger that drew people together for the lengthy struggle ahead. A *Newsweek* headline read: "AMERICANS ALL: National Disunity is Ended." A University of Oregon student declared: "We're all together now; that ought to be worth a couple of battleships."

Americans, John Morton Blum (*V Was for Victory*) has suggested, were largely in agreement on their aims in the war. Victory was, without question, the preeminent concern of policymakers and the public alike, yet there were other, more specific aims to which most people subscribed. Even before the United States entered the war, in a message to Congress in early 1941, FDR had spoken of the "four essential human freedoms"—freedom of

speech and expression, freedom of worship, freedom from want, and freedom from fear. In the summer of that year, in the Atlantic Charter, Roosevelt and British Prime Minister Winston Churchill had laid out their vision of the postwar world, a vision in which the self-determination of nations, equal trading rights for all, and a system of general security would prevail.

Those declarations helped define the war's formal mission. But most Americans—at home as well as on the battlefield—fought the war for more personal ends. Though they wanted to defeat the dictators—from Hitler to Hirohito—they saw the struggle not simply in ideological terms but within the framework of their own lives. They clung to a vision of home above all else as they struggled to make their way of life secure. John Hersey, a war correspondent, while reporting on marines on Guadalcanal, asked one young soldier why he was fighting. The G.I. paused for a moment, then responded, "Jesus, what I'd give for a piece of blueberry pie." For Hersey, that comment reflected both nostalgia and a commitment to home: soldiers, like others, were committed to the patterns they knew best. They were fighting to preserve what they most valued; they wanted a better past.

Americans saw the war in black and white terms. In 1942, anthropologist Margaret Mead observed that for people in the United States to make the necessary commitment, "we must feel that we are on the side of the Right." During the war, Americans felt that virtue was on their side. James Covert, a nine year old from Portland, Oregon, when the war began, later recalled his view of the struggle: "To me it was like a medieval morality play. They were bad, we were good, and God was on our side." Poet and Librarian of Congress Archibald MacLeish was more eloquent. For him, the war was "in its essence a revolt of man against himself—a revolt of stunted, half-formed, darkened men against a human world beyond their reach and most of all against the human world of reason and intelligence and sense."

Within that framework, soldiers fighting overseas sometimes seemed larger than life to the folks back home. While only 1 out of 3 men between the ages of 17 and 35 served in the armed forces, there were still approximately 16 million men in uniform during

the war, and they received special attention for their role in the struggle. Reporters and writers portrayed both generals and lowly G.I.s in heroic terms. Whether they came from small towns or big cities, they represented the best qualities in American life. Millions of Americans read the dispatches of Ernie Pyle, collected today by editor David Nichols in *Ernie's War: The Best of Ernie Pyle's World War II Dispatches* (1986), and with him applauded the soldiers' efforts to survive the wretched conditions they faced. While the military services censored the images from the battle front and so provided a sanitized picture of the war, Pyle gave his readers a real sense of the brutality of the struggle. Simple sentences—such as "The front-line soldier has lived like an animal for months and is a veteran of the cruel fierce world of death"—summed up the relentless difficulties ordinary soldiers faced and brought them closer to loved ones at home. More recent accounts, such as Paul Fussell's book *Wartime* and Stephen Spielberg's film *Saving Private Ryan* (1998), have given audiences an even more vivid sense of what the soldiers endured.

Journalists were not the only creators of heroic images. The United States conveyed its wartime goals through an organized propaganda program, described first by Allan M. Winkler in *The Politics of Propaganda: The Office of War Information, 1942–1945* (1978), that focused on securing support both at home and abroad. Propaganda provided a means through which the nation praised its people and defined its priorities for others around the world. Yet the program suffered from the same administrative difficulties that characterized other efforts in the Roosevelt government: an overlap of agencies constantly competing with one another, conflicting lines of authority, and general chaos until the middle of 1942.

From the time war broke out in Europe, Roosevelt tried first one propaganda measure, then another, just as he had on the mobilization front. An Office of Government Reports, established in September 1939, acted as a clearinghouse for requests for material from the government about its activities. The Division of Information of the Office of Emergency Management, set up in March 1941, served as the chief source of information about the gov-

ernment's defense activities. When neither of those agencies functioned well, the president created an Office of Facts and Figures—superimposed on both agencies—in October 1941, under the direction of Archibald MacLeish. Its purpose was to coordinate the presentation of materials pertaining to national defense. On the overseas front, playwright Robert Sherwood established a Foreign Information Service in the Office of the Coordinator of Information in August of the same year.

These sporadic efforts left the propaganda program in a state of shambles in the first months of America's formal involvement in the war. To deal with the chaos, in June 1942 Roosevelt finally created a new Office of War Information (OWI), which assumed the functions of all the other, earlier organizations. Heading the agency was news commentator Elmer Davis, a man known to millions of Americans for his clear delivery and dry humor in his nightly radio broadcasts on CBS.

Although OWI ran into resistance from the start—particularly from Republicans who viewed it as a publicity arm to promote a fourth term for FDR—it did manage to convey the nation's aims in the war. It trumpeted the liberal terms of the Four Freedoms and the Atlantic Charter. Even more important, it reflected the war Americans were fighting by describing American values and portraying Americans as they wanted to be seen. In the view that OWI conveyed, Americans—soldiers and civilians alike—were sympathetic, even sentimental. They combined "an idealistic aspiration toward Utopia with shrewd, hard, horse sense. . . . They are slow to anger, but, once aroused, they finish what they start." Americans were, according to OWI, "an aggressive people, tough and virile—who can take the initiative, who hit hard and like to hit hard." Having conquered a continent, they were now ready to conquer their enemies in the war.

OWI pictured American society in flattering ways. Through radio messages, leaflets, booklets, and films, it described the industrial miracles taking place as the United States created the greatest fighting machine ever known. *Victory*, a glossy OWI magazine, told of one factory producing a four-engine bomber every hour as it let the world know that 2 million men would soon

fight in 185,000 American planes. OWI's film *Autobiography of a Jeep* told in 16 different languages the story of the vehicle that came to symbolize American involvement in the war wherever it went.

Propaganda constantly sought to generate an appreciation for the American way of life. OWI issued stories on everything from ballet to baseball. It showed Americans engaged in such diverse activities as fighting boll weevils, governing themselves, and going to church. The treatment was overwhelmingly positive. There were obvious faults in American society, to be sure. But even while reporting problems to the rest of the world, OWI slanted them so that the larger picture remained hopeful as it portrayed the America that ordinary citizens wanted to protect.

And in all the material it issued, OWI communicated the sense of confidence that Americans felt. In his message asking for a declaration of war after Pearl Harbor, Franklin Roosevelt proclaimed his abiding faith that "we will gain the inevitable triumph—so help us God." OWI echoed that faith. Its basic message, according to Elmer Davis, was "that we are coming, that we are going to win, and that in the long run everybody will be better off because we won."

OWI was not the only organization trying to generate support for the war effort. An Office of Civilian Defense (OCD) was similarly involved in trying to boost American morale, even as it sought to protect civilians from attack by involving them in civil defense programs. Set up in May 1941 under the direction of New York Mayor Fiorello La Guardia, OCD worked in a variety of ways to encourage participation in the war. La Guardia was most interested in the air raid protection side of his organization. Even before Pearl Harbor, he moved to set up local defense councils in cities and towns, but that early program was barely adequate. After the Japanese strike, however, Americans grew fearful of further attacks: they saw German submarines cruising off the East Coast, and they were aware of Japanese submarine activity off the West Coast. In a February 1942 press conference, the president fueled those fears when he responded to a question about the possibility of an enemy attack. The enemy, he replied, "can come in and shell New York tomorrow night, under certain conditions. They can

probably . . . drop bombs on Detroit tomorrow night, under certain conditions." In the months that followed, the civil defense effort became more systematic and began to bring results. Cities participated in blackouts to protect themselves from possible attack, and volunteer ground observers scanned the skies for enemy planes.

Air raid protection, however, was only a part of OCD's mandate. Roosevelt also intended the agency to boost morale. A Voluntary Participation Program, directed by Eleanor Roosevelt, the president's wife, soon ran into trouble. Mrs. Roosevelt appointed Mayris Chaney, a dancer, and Melvyn Douglas, a liberal and outspoken actor, to her staff. Political opponents attacked Chaney as a "fan dancer" and "stripteaser" and Douglas as a fellow traveler and communist sympathizer. In the face of those attacks, Mrs. Roosevelt and her associates resigned.

Yet OCD continued to encourage citizen involvement in the struggle. In the spring of 1942, it sponsored a series of "town meetings for war," staged presentations that were aimed at promoting participation. It also supported the numerous campaigns that sought to motivate home-front Americans to do their part in the war.

Campaigns and Popular Culture

These campaigns, first described in detail by Richard R. Lingeman in *Don't You Know There's a War On? The American Home Front, 1941–1945* (1970), took many forms. Seeking to channel civilian energies into useful tasks, the government encouraged people to save scarce resources whenever they could. Homemakers, for example, were cajoled to save kitchen fats and turn them in to the local butcher. One pound of fat presumably contained enough glycerin to manufacture a pound of black powder that could be used for bullets or shells.

Americans likewise followed instructions about saving scarce metals. If each American family bought one less tin can a week, the argument went, the nation would save 2,500 tons of tin and 1,900 tons of steel, which in turn could be used to produce 5,000 tanks or 38 Liberty ships. The iron in one old shovel could be converted into four hand grenades. Razor blades contained steel that

could be recycled and made into machine guns; old lipstick tubes contained brass that could be reused in cartridges. Eager to play their part, citizens collected old tin cans and other objects for the popular scrap drives. In Virginia, they raised sunken ships from the James River. In Wyoming, they dismantled an old steam engine and then built an access road to permit parts collection.

When rubber was in short supply, people gathered materials that could be reused. In June 1942, the president asked people at home to collect "old tires, old rubber raincoats, old garden hoses, rubber shoes, bathing caps, gloves—whatever you have that is made of rubber." Some got caught up in the spirit of the drive. The manager of a radio station in New York voiced his delight when "a carload of girls from a musical comedy drove up here and they busted off garter straps, wriggled out of girdles and what not. This is fun!" he declared.

Still another campaign encouraged Americans to buy bonds to help finance the war. In the spring of 1941, Roosevelt permitted a campaign initiated by Secretary of the Treasury Henry Morgenthau, Jr., "to use *bonds* to sell the *war*." On September 21, 1943, singer Kate Smith played her part in a radio drive. Speaking 65 times between 8:00 A.M. and 2:00 A.M. the next morning to an audience of some 20 million people, she raised about $39 million.

Other bond drives followed. The seven war loans were all oversubscribed, though government officials were disappointed that individual quotas went unfilled while institutions—banks and corporations—took up the slack. In their effort to encourage individual involvement and investment, organizers often resorted to promotional stunts. Auctioneers traded celebrity items—actor Jack Benny's violin, actress Betty Grable's stockings, racehorse Man O' War's shoes—in return for pledges to buy bonds.

On still another front, government propagandists encouraged Americans to plant "victory gardens" in order to supply a portion of their own food. That program was enormously popular and, at its height, resulted in nearly 20 million such gardens. Some consisted of large fields; others were tiny plots. In 1943, these gardens provided more than one-third of all the vegetables grown in the country. Some people experimented with different kinds of

crops, and new foods such as Swiss chard and kohlrabi found their way onto American tables.

Not all victory gardens were successful, but it was the spirit that counted. Sheril Jankovsky Cunning, who grew up in Long Beach, California, during the war, recalled her family's garden: "We had the most miserable, hard-as-cement, three-by-five-foot plot of ground, and grew radishes and carrots as our contribution to the war. But radishes weren't anybody's mainstay, and our carrots never got bigger than an inch. Yet we all wanted to do our part for the war. You got caught up in the mesmerizing spirit of patriotism."

Conserve and collect. Play your part. Do what was necessary to support the war. In drive after drive, Americans were encouraged to "Use it up, wear it out, make it do or do without." Those who resisted or proved reluctant were bound to be rebuked by the popular refrain, "Don't you know there's a war on?"

Most home-front Americans, as Richard Polenberg (*War and Society*) and Geoffrey Perrett (*Days of Sadness, Years of Triumph: The American People, 1939–1945*, 1973) have shown, were comfortable during the war. They shared a feeling of well-being that had been missing a decade earlier. Demographic patterns reflected their improved mood. Working at well-paying jobs once again, young people who had chosen to postpone marriage or family during the depression now wed. Population, which had grown by only 3 million in the 1930s, increased by 6.5 million between 1940 and 1945; the postwar baby boom actually began during the war.

Popular music trumpeted American optimism. "Goodbye, Momma, I'm off to Yokohama," proclaimed one song. "Praise the Lord and Pass the Ammunition," echoed another. "There's a Star Spangled Banner Waving Somewhere" was one of the best-selling records in the country in 1942 and 1943. Americans seeking a song like "Over There," which had so captured their eagerness and summed up their confidence in World War I, never found one. Instead, the music industry ground out a series of trite and forgettable titles, including: "You're a Sap, Mister Jap"; "Let's Take a Rap at the Jap"; "The Japs Don't Have a Chinaman's Chance"; and "We're Gonna Find a Feller Who Is Yeller and Beat Him Red, White, and Blue." The sentimental favorite had nothing to do with

fighting or with the war itself. "White Christmas," first heard in 1942 in the film *Holiday Inn*, was soon sung by soldiers in hot desert jungles as well as by civilians in the United States. Like blueberry pie, the song represented home.

Americans, working at full tilt during the war, sought new ways to spend the money that once again lined their pockets. They could now afford items they had done without in the depression years, only to find out that much of what they wanted was in short supply as the country converted to the production of war goods. Some saved their money, as evidenced by bank deposits reaching a new high; others paid off mortgages and debts; and still others found new ways to dispose of new income.

"People want to spend money," a store manager noted, "and if they can't spend it on textiles they'll spend it on furniture; or . . . we'll find something else for them." In 1942, Americans spent $95 million on pharmaceuticals, $20 million more than the year before. They were no sicker; they simply had money to spare. The average department store sale rose from $2 before the war to $10 during the struggle. On December 7, 1944—the third anniversary of Pearl Harbor—R. H. Macy & Company in New York enjoyed the biggest selling day in its history.

People bought books in greater numbers. Paper was in short supply, so publishers used smaller type and issued fewer titles. Even so, book sales rose as a mass market developed. Every year after Pearl Harbor, the number of books sold rose by more than 20 percent. Publishers in 1943 did 40 percent better than the year before; membership in the Book-of-the-Month Club doubled during the war.

A new market for paperback books—introduced in 1939 by the Pocket Book Company—also developed at this time. Paperback sales increased astronomically, jumping from several hundred thousand to 10 million units in 1941, then rising to 20 million in 1942 and 40 million in 1943. Avon and Dell, like Pocket Books, capitalized on the growing demand. Murder mysteries were the most popular titles—150,000 sold per week—with self-help and health books coming next.

The publishing phenomenon of the war was *One World* by Wendell Willkie, defeated Republican presidential candidate in

1940. His book, issued in the fall of 1943 after he returned from a tour of the Soviet Union, China, the Middle East, and North and South America, was a plea for harmony and a call for hope in the postwar world. It sold faster than any book in publishing history. Simon and Schuster had anticipated selling 200,000 copies, only to find that the first printing was gone in 72 hours. One million copies—both hardbound and softbound—sold in two months; two million copies sold in two years. "*One World* was probably the most influential book published in America during the war," wrote one reviewer. "Like *Uncle Tom's Cabin* it was part of the country."

Americans also enjoyed comic books. Comic book sales rose from 12 million copies a month in 1942 to over 60 million a month in 1946. Eighty percent of the population aged 6 to 17 read comic books during the war; one-third of people aged 18 to 30 years did the same. Seventy million people followed their heroes in daily newspaper comic strips. Publishers catered to both a children's and a servicemen's market; a special edition of *Superman* went overseas.

The subject matter of most comics, like books and other forms of entertainment, reflected common concerns. Americans continued to be amused by the antics of comic book characters, as they had been in the past, and enjoyed watching them confront many of the same problems real people faced every day.

Most comic heroes participated in the war: Joe Palooka, Dick Tracy, and others enlisted in the military services and did their part. But not all characters became involved on the fighting front. Superman sat out the war, for his creators worried that he would make the struggle seem too easy, especially considering the hardships faced by real soldiers. Reporter Clark Kent, therefore, was 4-F for the duration: at his preinduction physical, he failed the eye test when his X-ray vision led him to read the chart in the next room. On other fronts, "Blondie" and "Bringing Up Father" poked fun at the problems of wartime life and encouraged participation in bond and conservation campaigns. Wonder Woman, a new creation in 1941, sought "to save the world from the hatred and wars of men in a man-made world," as she provided a different kind of role model for the nation's young.

During the war, Americans went to the movies in record numbers. Hollywood prospered, as Bernard F. Dick (*The Star-Spangled Screen: The American World War II Film*, 1985), Clayton R. Koppes and Gregory D. Black (*Hollywood Goes to War: How Politics, Profits and Propaganda Shaped World War II Movies*, 1987), and John Whiteclay Chambers, II and David Culbert (*World War II, Film, and History*, 1996) have shown. More than 90 million people attended films each week as admissions increased about 33 percent. Yearly grosses at theaters swelled to well over a billion dollars, even though fears of film stock shortages caused the total number of pictures released to drop from 533 in 1942 to 377 in 1945.

During the conflict, Hollywood continued to grind out the entertainment stories that had been popular in peacetime. Some critics, Archibald MacLeish among them, complained that the films were "escapist and delusive," and failed to address the issues of the war. They argued that light musicals like *Star Spangled Rhythm* or *The Yanks Are Coming* showed no sensitivity to larger questions, and that battle pictures like *Stand by for Action* conveyed nothing more than the value of military strength. *Casablanca*, the still-popular Humphrey Bogart and Ingrid Bergman film, critics argued, buried ideological concerns beneath the protagonist Rick's cynicism and paid more attention to romantic issues. The critics were right, but Hollywood persisted, for its winning formula remained popular during the war.

Americans also spent money on other forms of entertainment. They joined country clubs and golf clubs; they went to racetracks; they frequented nightclubs in increasing numbers. The entertainment business boomed, despite liquor shortages and a federal amusement tax. Big bands were similarly popular. So, too, were performers like Frank Sinatra, a young crooner from Hoboken, New Jersey, who became a sensation. In 1942, at New York's Paramount Theater, huge audiences of bobby-soxers—young teenage girls wearing socks rolled to the ankle—swooned as their hero sang.

Vacations were more popular than in the decade before. Americans swarmed to crowded bus depots and train stations as they left for an out-of-town holiday. East, West, and Gulf coast beaches

were crowded in the summer, and destination resorts in Florida were equally popular in the winter. Those who chose not to vacation far from home found new attractions and amusements nearby.

Americans remained intensely interested in professional sports. Baseball, the national game, was hurt by the war when more than 4,000 of the 5,700 players in the major and minor leagues entered the military services. Still, the game survived. The president recognized its value as a morale builder and encouraged its continuation throughout the war.

The major leagues hung on. Games were played in twilight to allow working fans to attend without violating the ban on night contests that existed in some parts of the country. Teams often featured rosters dramatically different from those in the days before Pearl Harbor. Gone to the armed services were Joe DiMaggio, Bob Feller, Ted Williams, Hank Greenberg, Peewee Reese, and scores of others. Instead, lineups featured virtual unknowns. One such player was Pete Gray, who joined the St. Louis Browns in 1945. He played in seventy-seven games and hit .218—all with one arm. An able outfielder who caught the ball in his glove, then flipped it up, grabbed it with his bare hand, and threw it back, he could also lay down a good drag bunt. Crowds came to see Gray, who became a major box office attraction.

Crowds likewise came to see the All-American Girls Professional Baseball League after its formation in 1943. Created by Philip Wrigley, owner of the Chicago Cubs who wanted to maintain interest in baseball, the All-American Girls League began with four teams: the Rockford Peaches, the Racine Belles, the Kenosha Comets, and the South Bend Blue Sox. Featured many years later in the film *A League of Their Own* (1992), it doubled in size and eventually included 600 women who captured the imagination of Midwestern fans excited by the game.

Shortages and Controls

The war also brought problems at home. Americans, even those with money in their pockets, had to endure the disruptions that war created. While conditions in the United States were far more stable

than those in England, France, Germany, or the Soviet Union, they were troublesome nonetheless, particularly in boom times, and Americans were often frustrated by difficulties they could not avoid.

Shortages in consumer items irritated everyone. With raw materials diverted to military use, civilians had to make do with less in virtually every area of daily life. Cutbacks even affected clothing styles. Metal for zippers went into guns, rubber for girdles was used to make parts for trucks and tanks, and fabric for civilian clothing was needed for uniforms. Curtailment was therefore necessary in the number and kinds of clothing styles offered the public.

In March 1942, the War Production Board entered the field of fashion. Anxious to save 40 to 50 million pounds of wool a year, the WPB ordered the elimination of vests, patch pockets, cuffs, and an extra pair of trousers in men's suits. It also insisted that suits be single-breasted and feature slightly shorter jackets with narrower lapels. Women's fashions changed as well. Similar government regulations limited the width and length of skirts, which sent hemlines higher. Styles featured straighter cuts and simpler lines, without ruffles or pleats. Gone were the bathing suits with billowing skirts of the 1930s; two-piece suits were justified on the basis of military need. Fashion retailer Stanley Marcus called the new styles "patriotic chic."

Because silk was a war casualty, there were shortages in women's stockings. In 1941, the government embargoed silk that came from Japan. Nylon, used in about 20 percent of all hose, was substituted until that too was diverted, in this case into the manufacture of parachutes. Although cotton stockings existed, they never became popular, and, in any event, cotton too was scarce. Some women resorted to the not wholly satisfactory expedient of painting stockings on their legs.

Food shortages also bothered Americans. Sugar became scarce as early as December 1941, when imports from the Philippines stopped and shipping shortages hindered the transport of crops from Cuba and Puerto Rico. People began to hoard sugar immediately after Pearl Harbor. Even when supplies of Caribbean sugar became available, they failed to keep up with civilian and military demand. A coffee shortage occurred when lack of cargo

space prevented its transport from Brazil. Meats and countless other items were similarly in short supply.

Throughout the country, people struggled to make do. They cut back on the amount of sugar they used in food or drink and learned to use sugar substitutes for cooking and baking. Restaurants put less sugar in sugar bowls. To meet the coffee crisis, some establishments began cutting out coffee refills and railroad dining cars served coffee only at breakfast. Meat shortages led some restaurants to bolster their menus by offering buffalo or antelope steaks—even beaverburgers—as alternatives to more traditional fare.

While the shortages themselves hurt, the larger government concern was that severe demand would lead to price increases. The rapidly increasing federal spending was putting more and more money in circulation, prompting real fears that inflation would spiral out of control. And the fears seemed warranted: in the first half of 1942, the cost-of-living index climbed 7 percent. When Roosevelt received the advice that "a little inflation would not hurt," he responded with the story of "a fellow who took a little cocaine and kept coming back for more until he was a drug addict." He remembered World War I, when prices had risen 62 percent between 1914 and 1918 and another 40 percent in the immediate postwar years. And the president was determined not to allow another such spurt.

FDR first attempted to head off inflationary woes when he created the Office of Price Administration and Civilian Supply in April 1941. John Kenneth Galbraith ("Reflections on Price Control," *Quarterly Journal of Economics*, 1949) was one of the first scholars to describe the difficulties that agency faced. Charged with preventing profiteering and price hiking, which could raise the cost of living, the office had only the power of "jawboning"—trying to force compliance by verbal argument alone—and proved ineffective. The following January, Congress gave the agency, now called simply the Office of Price Administration (OPA), the power to freeze retail prices and control rents in areas near war plants. When this process of selective controls proved cumbersome, OPA in April 1942 issued the General Maximum Price Regulation, which froze retail prices at the level they had reached in March.

Though that ruling too was hard to enforce, it opened the way for another measure in October of the same year that further broadened price control and provided for wage control as well.

OPA also got into the business of rationing, with ten national programs that began in 1942. Rationing came to include such scarce items as sugar, coffee, meat, butter, tires, and gasoline. Ration books, issued by local boards, contained stamps or coupons entitling consumers to purchase different products that were in short supply. Initially, the system worked on a single-item basis; later, it was revised to include a flexible point system that could be adjusted to deduct more points for particularly scarce items. The revised system was developed in an effort to bring supply in line with demand.

Consumers grumbled about the rationing program, which seemed to violate the traditional American value of individual choice. Moreover, the rules felt overly restrictive. Some people therefore resorted to the black market, where they had to pay a bit more but could usually get what they wanted from an agreeable merchant. Black market operations were illegal, of course, but nonetheless involved even respectable proprietors and flourished as Americans struggled with the inconveniences at home.

Despite the complaints, price control worked. Scarce goods were distributed relatively fairly, and inflation was held in check. In the two years after mid-1943, consumer prices rose by less than 2 percent. Though OPA was one of the most unpopular federal agencies, Gallup polls revealed that more than 90 percent of the public approved of some form of price control.

Americans were less sympathetic toward wage control. Workers were unhappy when wages did not seem to keep pace with profits. Though wages did rise during the war, thanks in large part to overtime efforts, the gap between wages and profits seemed to grow larger all the time.

Organized labor, Nelson Lichtenstein has observed in *Labor's War at Home*, was particularly unhappy with the regulatory apparatus that placed restrictions on what employees could earn. The president was concerned that wage increases as much as price increases would fuel inflation. Wages, therefore, had to stay within

certain bounds. The National War Labor Board (NWLB), the organization responsible for wage control, adopted what was known as the "Little Steel" formula in July 1942. Faced with a wage demand by workers at the Bethlehem, Republic, Youngstown, and Inland steel companies, the NWLB established a formula for wage increases. It took January 1, 1941, as a starting point, then allowed a 15 percent increase to meet the rise in living costs until May 1942. The formula was applied in other war-related industries as well and served to keep inflation in check.

The NWLB retained some discretionary authority to correct inequities, but it lost that authority with the president's "hold the line" order in April 1943. When labor protested the provision that wage hikes were no longer to be considered in collective bargaining, some modification of the Little Steel formula was permitted, but the basic outlines of the policy remained intact and held the rise in wage rates to only 24 percent throughout the war.

Organized labor was all the more troubled because labor and business representatives together had agreed on December 23, 1941, to refrain from strikes and lockouts. Made as a patriotic gesture, the "no-strike" pledge was non-binding, but nevertheless had the force of a moral commitment. The pledge became more difficult to sustain as living costs rose. In mid-1943, the Michigan CIO voted to rescind the pledge. The issue had surfaced in 1942, at which time it had been defeated; the next year the outcome was reversed. Though the vote in one state brought no nationwide change, it reflected growing worker dissatisfaction.

And many workers, in fact, often simply ignored the pledge. Militancy from below led to wildcat strike activity that increased steadily during the war. The number of strikes and strikers in 1942 was roughly consistent with depression-years numbers. It more than doubled in 1943 and continued to rise in 1944 and 1945. Altogether, there were 14,471 strikes throughout the country between the time of the attack on Pearl Harbor and the end of the war with Japan. The problem peaked in 1944, with more than 2,115,000 workers idle and roughly 8,721,000 workdays lost. Most of the work stoppages were short, lasting only a few days. Nonetheless, they disturbed government officials. "Strikes

are spreading at an alarming rate," declared one NWLB member, "and unless they are checked immediately, the 'no-strike—no lockout' agreement will become meaningless."

The most disturbing strikes came in the coal fields. John L. Lewis, head of the United Mine Workers, was a bitter enemy of FDR. Lewis, as Melvyn Dubofsky and Warren Van Tine have shown (*John L. Lewis: A Biography*, 1977), was an outspoken leader. Though he had initially supported both the New Deal and the president, in the late 1930s he became disillusioned with what he felt was FDR's overly cautious approach to reform. He opposed Roosevelt's reelection in 1940, and remained determined to advance the interests of his own men. The president had no affection for Lewis either. In late 1941, he termed him a "psychopathic" case, and two years later said that he would be happy to resign if Lewis would commit suicide.

In 1943, Lewis led 400,000 bituminous coal miners in strikes on four different occasions. He claimed that the miners had long worked for substandard wages and in substandard conditions. "When the mine workers' children cry for bread," he declared, "they cannot be satisfied with a 'Little Steel' formula." It was a "miserably stupid" arrangement, issued by a board of "labor zombies." He therefore demanded substantial wage concessions.

When management refused to budge, Lewis called three successive walkouts, each lasting several days, in May and June. The government then took control over the mines, with Secretary of the Interior Ickes in charge. Each time there was a walkout, work resumed after the administration appealed to the miners' patriotism and threatened at the same time to end draft deferments for those who stayed out on strike.

Lewis was not popular but he was persistent. Though polls in June 1943 showed that 87 percent of the public viewed him unfavorably, he had unanimous rank and file support. In early November, when all bituminous coal miners were again on strike, Roosevelt once more seized the mines, but this time he ordered Ickes to negotiate a contract acceptable to Lewis. Ickes did so, reaching an agreement that bypassed the restrictions of the "Little Steel" formula. Lewis had won, though the formula remained in force in other industries until the end of the war.

The agitation in the coal fields, however, had consequences that affected the larger labor movement. Conservative elements in Congress, uncomfortable with the impressive labor gains of the 1930s, had been looking for an opportunity to limit any further labor advances. With business interests once again in control, the conservatives sensed a shift in political mood. When a dozen states passed measures that restricted labor in 1943, Congress was ready to act at the national level.

The War Labor Disputes Act, sponsored by Representative Howard Smith of Virginia and Senator Tom Connally of Texas and known as the Smith-Connally Act, was passed in June 1943. It required unions to give formal notice of intention to strike, to observe a 30-day cooling-off period, and then to gain majority membership approval before walking out. The act also gave the president greater power to seize war plants, imposed penalties on unions for engaging in illegal work stoppages, and prohibited union gifts to political campaigns. Although Roosevelt vetoed the measure, Congress overrode the veto within a few hours. While the Smith-Connally Act never proved as restrictive as its opponents feared, it did reflect a shift in sympathy at the national level. For many members of the workforce, it proved to be one more irritant during the war.

Wartime Dislocations

The war also brought other dislocations that disrupted stability at home. Record numbers of Americans—approximately 20 percent of the population—moved from one place to another during the struggle. Fifteen million crossed county lines; eight million moved across state lines. Some of the migrants were members of servicemen's families who, in an effort to stay together as long as possible, followed loved ones (in training camps and duty stations) until they were sent overseas. Others found their way to factories in different parts of the country where they helped make weapons of war.

Americans moved in all directions. Many drifted from south to north; more traveled from east to west. Since half of the nation's shipbuilding and airplane manufacturing activity took place on the

Pacific Coast, many of the migrants headed in that direction. As Richard White has shown in *"It's Your Misfortune and None of My Own": A New History of the American West* (1991), federal resources fueled the extraordinary development of the western United States. During the war years, the federal government invested almost $40 billion in factories, military bases, and other installations, and spent a total of $70 billion in the Southwest, Mountain West, and Far West. Such spending changed the configuration of national power. California attracted 2 million new inhabitants, with the population of the Los Angeles area alone growing by 440,000. By 1945, southern California had more people than the total of 37 other states. As White has noted, "It was as if someone had tilted the country: people, money, and soldiers all spilled west."

At the same time, other areas expanded as well. Michigan had a net increase of 287,000 people between 1940 and 1943, with many of the newcomers concentrated in the Detroit area, where workers were needed in converted automobile plants and airplane factories. Seaport regions in the South increased in size too. In the four years after 1940, the population of the Mobile, Alabama, area grew by 65 percent; the Hampton Roads, Virginia, area by 45 percent; and the Charleston, South Carolina, area by 38 percent. Washington, D.C., flooded with new government workers and dollar-a-year men, grew by 231,000 between 1940 and 1943.

Cities in particular suffered terrible congestion that proved hard to handle. Having been shaken by the often insurmountable demands of the Great Depression, many cities felt the strain even before they had geared up for war. Some cities still had debts to repay and long-overdue civic improvements to make. Now they had to cope with tens or even hundreds of thousands of new inhabitants in inadequate houses, hospitals, and schools.

Often, urban living conditions were grim. Housing developments were crowded and cramped, depressing to those who came from rural regions where they had been accustomed to open spaces. In the novel *The Dollmaker,* the Nevels family, having migrated from eastern Kentucky to Detroit, settled in a housing

project where one building looked just like the next, where families could hear one another through thin walls, where the bleak urban environment seemed a prison. Harriette Arnow described Gertie Nevels's reaction as the family arrived at its new home:

A few feet away across a strip of soot-blackened snow were four steps leading to a door with a glass top, set under low, icicle-fringed eaves. There was on either side of the door a little window; in front of one was a gray coal shed; in front of the other a telephone pole, and by it a gray short-armed cross. The door was one in a row of six, one other door between it and the railroad tracks. Gertie turned sharply away, and across the alley her glance met another door exactly like her own.

In some war-plant areas, particularly around Willow Run, workers who could not find more permanent housing lived in trailers with substandard sanitation and in constant fear of disease.

Worse than the unpleasant living conditions many migrants endured were the harsh responses of residents disgruntled by the waves of migrants spilling into their communities and disrupting their lives. Rural arrivals found themselves branded "hillbillies." Cruel tales circulated about southerners who arrived in Detroit without shoes or who dropped letters in fire alarm boxes. "Before the bomber plant was built, everything was perfect here," one Willow Run resident observed. "Everybody knew everybody else and all were happy and contented. Then came that bomber plant and all this influx of riffraff, mostly Southerners. You can't be sure of these people." The newcomers themselves were equally unhappy. "We found Detroit a cold city, a city without a heart or a soul," David Crockett Lee wrote to his local newspaper. "So we are going back to Tennessee . . . where men and women are neighborly, and where even the stranger is welcome."

Inadequate housing was perhaps the most serious urban issue. Even before the war began, many cities could not meet housing needs. A 1938 Works Progress Administration (WPA) survey, for example, revealed that 70,000 of Detroit's 414,000 dwelling units were substandard. With the huge population increase during the war, the situation became intolerable as municipal areas found it impossible to keep up with the influx of new arrivals. Condi-

tions were the same all over the country. In Hartford, Connecticut, 10,000 additional units were needed in 1942 alone.

Families were often reduced to living together in a single room. A San Francisco city official observed in 1943: "Families are sleeping in garages, with mattresses right on cement floors and three, four, five to one bed." Shantytowns, like the Hoovervilles of the Great Depression, sprang up, with inadequate sewage facilities and a lack of basic necessities.

The federal effort to build more housing became bogged down in bureaucratic disputes, best described in Philip J. Funigiello's *The Challenge to Urban Liberalism: Federal-City Relations during World War II* (1978). New Deal reformers wanted to use public housing to revitalize cities, abolish slums, and eliminate urban poverty. During the war, their priorities clashed with those of presidential appointees who wanted to build structures to accommodate new workers as quickly and expeditiously as possible. Congress came down on the side of speed, as fiscal conservatives had little sympathy with what they termed "socialistic experiments" and sought to ensure that public housing would not compete with private enterprise in the postwar period.

In the early months of the war, little progress was made in coping with the problem. Then, in February 1942, Roosevelt finally consolidated 16 different housing organizations into one National Housing Agency (NHA). The new agency soon decided on the construction of temporary structures, a policy that held for the duration of the war. Once underway, a great deal of building occurred. The government spent $2.3 billion in a massive construction effort, as the NHA erected 832,000 units to accompany the 1 million units built by private companies. The agency also located existing vacant housing for workers to rent when it could. While the effort did not wholly meet wartime needs, it did succeed in dealing with the most serious conditions.

Family stress was another problem during the war. Families suffered the strains of separation as soldiers went overseas and the strains of reconnecting when they returned. Some suffered even worse strains when loved ones were killed in combat. The Bureau of Labor Statistics estimated the breakup of more than 3 million

families by April 1944. The divorce rate rose from 16 per 100 marriages in 1940 to 27 per 100 in 1944. Never before—not even during the Great Depression—had American families been subjected to such stress.

Inadequate day-care facilities complicated the lives of working mothers. Shortages across the country, according to Karen Anderson, in *Wartime Women: Sex Roles, Family Relations, and the Status of Women during World War II* (1981), were severe. In Seattle, in late 1942, there were but seven WPA nurseries and three private establishments serving 350 children, with 75,000 women in the work force. In Tacoma, only one day-care center accommodated 20,000 women. The Lanham Act of 1940 provided federal funds to assist expanding war communities, but bureaucratic procedures were cumbersome and slow. Still, by the war's end, the government had spent $52 million on 3,102 centers for 600,000 children in the largest commitment to child care the nation had ever made. Though that hardly met the total need, it was a start. Yet even the provision of day-care facilities did not ensure their use. Some mothers were reluctant to put their children in institutional settings, so they worked out a variety of other makeshift arrangements.

"Latchkey children"—who returned after school to empty homes while their mothers were still at work—were a source of concern, particularly in the early years of the war. As William M. Tuttle, Jr., has shown vividly in *"Daddy's Gone to War": The Second World War in the Lives of America's Children* (1993), the war had a powerful and sometimes unsettling effect on children as well as adults.

With children on their own more, juvenile delinquency became a serious problem and truancy rates rose. In Detroit, the truancy rate jumped 24 percent between 1938 and 1943. High school enrollment across the country dropped by more than 1 million from 1941 to 1944. Juvenile crime rates rose, with theft, property damage, and sexual misconduct the major offenses.

Many Americans were even more worried about the unsavory actions of "victory girls"—young women who flaunted traditional moral codes and attached themselves to servicemen when they

could. While promiscuity was not as serious a problem as prostitution, it still disturbed those committed to conventional mores. In 1942, more than twice as many girls under the age of 21 were arrested for sexual offenses than in the year before.

Venereal disease was also a wartime problem, particularly among the young. The incidence of syphilis among young women aged 15 to 19 in New York City was 204 percent higher for a ten-month period in 1944 than for the corresponding period in 1941. New York had the image of "Sin City," but problems surfaced elsewhere as well. Terming syphilis and gonorrhea "enemy agents within our midst," reformers attacked prostitution. The May Act in 1941 allowed communities to close brothels near military establishments. By 1944, 700 cities had shut down their red-light districts. An internal war on vice was underway.

Other kinds of dislocations affected those with ethical or personal commitments at odds with the views of mainstream America. Conscientious objectors were among those who experienced great difficulties during the war. Although, as Richard Polenberg has shown in *War and Society,* the Selective Service Act of 1940 specified that no one was to serve as a combatant who "by reason of religious training and belief is conscientiously opposed to participation in war in any form," the guidelines were narrowly interpreted, making it difficult to gain such a designation. In civilian public service camps, where conscientious objectors could work in place of military service, objectors were subject to military discipline and paid no wages. Some 5,500 men who opposed the war on political and not religious grounds served time in jail. Ethical commitment extracted a high price.

One's sexual orientation could cause similar complications. Because the military defined homosexuality as deviant behavior, the United States screened for homosexuality during the induction process on the grounds that it rendered a recruit unfit for service. Yet procedures were often lax, and, as John D'Emilio (*Sexual Politics, Sexual Communities: The Making of a Homosexual Minority in the United States, 1940–1970,* 1983) and Allan Bérubé (*Coming Out under Fire: The History of Gay Men and Women in World War Two,* 1990) have noted, many gay men ended up pass-

ing the pre-induction test. Author Merle Miller, then seeking to conceal his own sexual orientation, later recalled, "I was afraid I would never get into the army, but after the psychiatrist tapped me on the knee with a little hammer and asked how I felt about girls, before I really had a chance to answer, he said 'Next' and I was being sworn in." Gay soldiers—male and female—served effectively in the military services during the war, and the experience provided many of them an opportunity for exploration and self-discovery.

Conclusion

For all of the hardships, the United States fared well in World War II. Almost 400,000 Americans were military casualties, and their loss profoundly affected families and friends at home. By contrast, the struggle left 2.8 million German soldiers and 7.5 million Soviet soldiers dead. With civilian losses added to military figures, an estimated 20 million Russians died during the war. The United States entered the conflict relatively late, was located far from the major battlefields, and enjoyed the benefits of a war-induced prosperity within its own borders. By the middle of the conflict, nearly seven out of ten Americans said they had not had to make any "real sacrifices" as a result of the war.

Confident and committed, Americans were willing to do their part. Secure in their mission, they felt that their efforts would make the world a better place. They believed in their approach—successful once again—and in their destiny as they did what was necessary to support the national effort. They grumbled about shortages and endured deprivations, yet they knew that things were far better than they had been a decade ago. Discomforts could be tolerated with the knowledge that one day the war would end. There were some exceptions, to be sure, for minority groups and women had a far more difficult time. But for most home-front Americans, World War II was an experience that changed their lives in positive ways.

CHAPTER THREE

Outsiders and Ethnic Groups

Not all Americans fared well in World War II. German Americans, now better assimilated, were more fortunate than they had been during World War I, when they had suffered hostile attacks at home because of their heritage. But the war posed problems for other groups outside the mainstream of American life. While the struggle opened new opportunities for employment and integration for some, other outsiders encountered serious disruptions in daily life that were difficult to overcome. Women, long relegated to inferior positions in the workforce, now found better jobs in record numbers, though they still experienced discrimination on various fronts. African Americans likewise seized on the enormous industrial expansion to press for better positions. Yet they too encountered various forms of resistance wherever they turned, and soon learned that true societal change came only in response to the application of constant pressure. While other groups, such as Latinos and American Indians, made some gains, they were not as well organized and enjoyed less conspicuous success. Italian Americans at first found themselves designated enemy aliens, though that label was lifted after a few years. The wartime experi-

ence was even worse for Japanese Americans, who faced the scorn of white friends and neighbors—and were then rounded up and incarcerated by the federal government. Meanwhile, American Jews, though safe themselves in the United States, were powerless to help as friends and relatives died in Hitler's concentration camps in Europe, as their own government failed to take actions that might have halted the genocide sooner.

All outsiders sensed the hypocrisy in the United States fighting for freedom and democracy overseas while turning a blind eye toward racial and sexual discrimination at home. Propaganda portrayed the war in idealistic terms that rang untrue to those still waiting to enjoy the benefits of the American dream. Outsiders protested the gap between the nation's pronouncements and its practices but worked all the while to use the demands of war to improve their own lot, thereby giving substance to the values guiding American involvement in the struggle.

Women and the War

The war brought enormous changes in American women's lives. Women were without question second-class citizens at the start of the conflict. They were particularly conscious of discrimination in the labor market. Numerous jobs were simply closed to them, which led to a concentration of working women in retail trade and domestic service. In those jobs they did hold, women were usually paid less than were men. During the Great Depression, conditions had worsened, as wives hoping to find work to help their struggling families confronted jobless men who keenly resented the new competition.

But the huge productive effort that began in 1940 gave women the chance to step outside commonly held positions as clerks and maids to do other kinds of work. Scholars such as Susan M. Hartmann (*The Home Front and Beyond: American Women in the 1940s*, 1982) and Karen Anderson (*Wartime Women*) have described in detail this influx of women into the workforce. Initially, industrial jobs remained closed to women. Unconvinced that supplies of male labor would be grossly depleted, employers were reluctant to modify their hiring practices. They also questioned whether

women had the physical strength or mechanical ability to handle industrial tasks. The War Department supported such attitudes with the assertion that defense firms "should not be encouraged to utilize women on a large scale until all available male labor in the area has first been employed."

But as millions of men entered the military services, the situation changed. From late 1942 on, both government and industry waged a concerted campaign to persuade women to work outside the home. The War Manpower Commission recruited women in areas where labor was scarce. The Office of War Information issued media appeals to women, the message stressing the excitement of working for good wages in a patriotic cause. One such advertisement in Seattle noted that "an American homemaker with the strength and ability to run a house and raise a family . . . has the strength and ability to take her place in a vital War industry." A Baltimore ad told women that war work was "a lot more exciting than polishing the family furniture."

Women eagerly responded. The number of working women rose from 14,600,000 in 1941 to 19,370,000 in 1944. In the latter year, 37 percent of all adult women were in the labor force. Since some women left jobs for personal reasons—even as aggregate totals grew—almost 50 percent of all women were employed at some point during 1944. At the peak of the industrial effort, women constituted 36 percent of the civilian workforce.

The demographic composition of the female part of the labor pool shifted. The most significant change, according to William Chafe in his path-breaking account, *The American Woman: Her Changing Social, Economic, and Political Roles, 1920–1970* (1972), came among married women. Traditionally, working women had been single and young. Between 1940 and 1944, married women accounted for 72.2 percent of the total number of new female employees, and, for the first time in American history, outnumbered single women in the female labor force. Women with absent husbands were twice as likely as others to work; half of all servicemen's wives were employed. Older women too began to work more, as more than 2 million women over the age of 35 found jobs. By the end of the war, half of all female workers were over 35.

Even more significant were the changes in the types of positions open to women. Some joined the military services, as noted in a book edited by Paula Nassen Poulos, *A Woman's War Too: U.S. Women in the Military in World War II* (1996). By the end of the war, more than 300,000 women had served in uniform. Recruitment played upon women's patriotism. Oveta Culp Hobby, head of the Women's Army Auxiliary Corps (WAAC—later shortened to WAC, Women's Army Corps) told potential recruits, "This is *your* war," in encouraging them to join. As personnel needs mounted, army officials were willing to use women in virtually all areas except combat. They served not only as clerks and typists, but also as radio operators, parachute riggers, and mechanics. The navy had a similar organization, Women Accepted for Volunteer Emergency Service (WAVES), and used one-quarter of all female recruits in naval aviation. Women Air Force Service Pilots (WASPs) ferried planes around the United States and towed targets for anti-aircraft gunnery practice sessions as well.

In the civilian sector, the most significant shift in women's work patterns was the move out of domestic service and into manufacturing. Between 1940 and 1944, the number of women in manufacturing rose 141 percent; their share of manufacturing positions increased from 22 percent to 32.7 percent. Women were particularly active in the defense industries. In Detroit, Ford and other automobile companies finally agreed to hire women for production work. By February 1943, women made up 90.8 percent of the new workers hired in 185 war plants in that city. Elsewhere, they entered shipyard production work; by 1943, they filled 10 percent of those jobs. Women also served as steelworkers, riveters, welders, and surface miners.

Other opportunities opened as well. Women's share of government jobs increased from 19.4 percent to 38.4 percent between 1940 and 1944. They worked for newspapers and radio stations in increasing numbers. Orchestra positions became available, as did positions on the stock exchange. In countless areas, the war made a major difference in the kinds of jobs women could hope to find.

And employers were glad to hire the women. Not only did they help take up the slack in a time of need, but they performed certain jobs particularly well. Some employers believed that

women could squeeze into tight places more easily than men, making them better welders of certain items. Others made the sexist assumption that women were better at repetitious and monotonous jobs than were men.

Men were not always comfortable with the changes they saw taking place. They feared that wartime demands might undermine femininity and give rise to a new class of masculine (or at least independent) women. Columnist Max Lerner voiced his concern that the war was developing a "new Amazon" who would "outdrink, outswear, and outswagger the men." When measures were pending to create women's service divisions, opponents revealed the nature of the threat they perceived. "What has become of the manhood of America, that we have to call on our women to do what has ever been the duty of men?" one asked. A Marine Corps officer, when informed that women were being sent to his camp, was even more blunt. "Goddamn it all," he was said to have exploded. "First they send us dogs. Now it's women."

Naturally, opponents of women's advances were most worried about the disruption of the traditional social and sexual order, where men worked and women were confined to the home—with all the domestic work this implied. If women worked, who would take their places in seeing that everything got done around the house? "Who will do the cooking, the washing, the mending, the humble homey tasks to which every woman has devoted herself; who will rear and nurture the children. . . ?" one legislator asked.

The concern over the welfare of children reflected a real problem. More than half a million women with children under the age of ten found jobs, but, as mentioned in Chapter Two, day-care facilities were in short supply. Moreover, the prevailing assumption remained that a mother's primary duty was to her home and children. The Children's Bureau declared that group care for children under two would cause "slower mental development, social ineptness, weakened initiative, and damage to the child's capacity. . . to form satisfactory relationships." But the War Manpower Commission, concerned about labor shortages, insisted that employers not discriminate against women with children, arguing that women should be free to decide for themselves if they wanted to work.

And so women worked, even as they continued to do traditional household chores and care for their children.

Women themselves shared some of the fears men voiced. They worried about their children even as they arranged whatever alternate care they could. They also worried about their own femininity in their new places of work. In this case, the media helped ease women's fears. Newspaper accounts, magazine stories, advertisements, and posters all portrayed women as glamorous employees pursuing patriotic tasks: they could be simultaneously gorgeous and productive. Grease-stained overalls need not hide the "real woman" underneath.

Everywhere the story was the same. As Alan Clive ("Women Workers in World War II: Michigan as a Test Case," *Labor History,* 1979) and Antonette Chambers Noble ("Utah's Rosies: Women in the Utah War Industries during World War II," *Utah Historical Quarterly,* 1991) have shown in studies of two different states, the basic pattern was nationwide. Every woman riveting at the N. A. Woodworth Company looked "like a cross between a campus queen and a Hollywood starlet," according to an article in the *Detroit News.* A *McCall's* magazine story about women workers told readers: "You'll like this girl. She does a man's work in the ground crew, servicing airplanes, but she hasn't lost any of her feminine sweetness and charm." *Life* magazine featured a photograph of Boeing employee Marguerite Kershner, noting in a caption that "although Marguerite looks like a Hollywood conception of a factory girl, she and thousands like her are doing hard, vital work." The famous images of "Rosie the Riveter" underscored the theme that beauty need not be lost in the accomplishment of vital tasks. Rosie had strong arms and wore overalls in a Norman Rockwell cover for the *Saturday Evening Post,* but she was comely and attractive nonetheless. Rosie, in all forms, became a national heroine to men and women alike.

Women, as Sherna Berger Gluck (*Rosie the Riveter Revisited: Women, the War, and Social Change* (1987), Maureen Honey (*Creating Rosie the Riveter: Class, Gender and Propaganda during World War II,* 1984), and editors Judy Barrett Litoff and David C. Smith (*American Women in a World at War: Contemporary Ac-*

counts from World War II, 1997) have demonstrated, were delighted to be employed. Financial considerations played a large part in their eagerness to work. Wives of servicemen suffered losses in income when their husbands went away, and employment helped them make up the difference, as well as ease the loneliness of separation. Many women, like Josephine McKee, a mother of nine who worked at the Boeing Aircraft Company in Seattle, used the income from war jobs to pay off debts acquired in bleaker times. Others, like Leola Houghland, a welder at Associated Shipyards (also in Seattle), used their earnings to pay for the family home. A number of women interviewed by the Women's Bureau noted that illness or disability of other family members required them to work.

Women who had no choice but to work were nonetheless pleased with the better opportunities now available. Evelyn Knight left her job as a cook to work in a navy yard saying, "After all, I've got to keep body and soul together, and I'd rather earn a living this way than to cook over a hot stove." Even when war-related jobs were monotonous and routine, they were more attractive—and better paying—than those women had held before.

Countless women found paid employment a welcome respite from keeping house. One working mother noted that the "companionship of working with others is vastly more stimulating and rewarding than housework" as she recalled the "narrowing effect that staying at home full time exerts upon my outlook in life." A Detroit government secretary declared, "[I] would just die if I had to stay home and keep house." Freda Philbrick, working at the Puget Sound Navy Yard, pointed out that "somehow the kitchen lacks the glamour of a bustling shipyard." One woman who remained at home observed of those who did not, "Some just love their jobs. I think they for the first time in their life feel important."

Patriotic considerations played an obvious part in women's willingness to work. They derived satisfaction from being able to do their part in the war. One rubber plant employee commented, "Every time I test a batch of rubber, I know it's going to help bring my three sons home quicker." Josephine Bucklin, a bus driver in Seattle acknowledged, "We do feel we're doing something con-

crete for the war effort." There was also an excitement, Bucklin noted, in doing "something women have never been allowed to do before."

Women felt an eagerness to prove they could do whatever was necessary. Adele Erenberg, a Los Angeles cosmetics clerk when the war started, went to work in a machine shop. Her first experience in the noisy room was intimidating, and two weeks passed before anyone spoke to her. Her response was: "Okay, you bastards, I'm going to prove to you I can do anything you can do, and maybe better than some of you." Helen Studer, who worked at Douglas Aircraft, observed that in working with such men, "You learned to swear like they did."

For all of the excitement, there was frequent frustration as well. Women constantly faced the kind of cold welcome Adele Erenberg received—particularly in positions formerly held only by men—and simply had to wait for coworkers' attitudes to change. Women also chafed under restrictions imposed by managers who were concerned about the mixing of the sexes in their plants. General Motors fired any male supervisor and female employee found "fraternizing." The company argued that questionable conduct by either party could hurt labor-management relations and compromise the policy of hiring women. Unions too imposed restrictions on women. Flint Local 599 of the United Automobile Workers voted that committeemen should ignore the grievances of any women "indecent in her wearing apparel or actions."

Worse still was the frustration that came from unfair pay differentials. Managerial positions, and the higher salaries they brought, were almost nonexistent for women. In other ways, too, women were paid less. Although the National War Labor Board ruled in the fall of 1942 that women who did "work of the same quality and quantity" as that of men should receive equal pay, the policy was not always fully implemented. Employers often assigned women to the lowest paying jobs in the plants. Since women had less seniority, managers could advance them more slowly and pay them correspondingly less. Moreover, managers continued to classify jobs as "men's" and "women's," with women's jobs paid at lower rates.

Simple figures tell the story. In the automobile industry in 1943, women averaged $44.91 per week, while men, whose work-week lasted only 3.5 hours longer, averaged $62.65. At the Ford Willow Run plant, women in the spring of 1945 earned $2,928 annually, compared to $3,363 for men.

Still, some gains occurred. Support for the principle of fairness grew in different quarters. The National Association of Manufacturers endorsed the idea of equal pay. Industries proved cooperative when the cost-plus contracts (described in Chapter One) allowed them to pay women more at no additional expense to themselves. Unions pressed for equal pay when women directly replaced men, although they failed to challenge discrimination when men and women worked in different jobs. By early 1944, the NWLB had heard from more than 2,200 companies that had eliminated discriminatory differentials, but the basic problem of unequal pay remained the norm.

For all of their involvement in the workforce, women, Susan M. Hartmann has suggested in *The Home Front and Beyond,* remained committed to traditional values during the war. Though they took advantage of new opportunities, they continued to feel as strong a commitment to marriage and family as they had before. The marriage rate rose, at least until the draft depleted the male population. Between 1940 and 1943, there were 1,118,000 more marriages than might have been expected. The number of children aged five years and under increased by 25 percent. And popular culture continued to stress the woman as wife and mother before all else.

Yet women flourished in their new positions, and many wanted to continue in them after the war. Surveys taken between 1943 and 1945 revealed that from 61 percent to 85 percent of the women working wanted to stay employed. For married women, the positive sentiments ran from 47 percent to 68 percent.

Women were not without ambivalence. While many of them may have enjoyed their experience in the workforce, they recognized the pressures that were soon to make it hard for them to stay on. As one woman who worked for the Naval Advance Depot in Tacoma noted: "My husband wants a wife, not a career woman." Others, however, either needed to continue in their jobs for finan-

Top: Women could play a major part in the war effort—and be attractive too—according to this famous poster. National Archives NWDNS-179-WP-1563

Middle: Woman worker applying the finishing touches to a flotation bag used to support airplanes forced down at sea. Courtesy Franklin D. Roosevelt Library

Bottom: Her mind is on her work—and on her country. A small flag tells the story for this worker at a midwest drill and tool company. Courtesy Franklin D. Roosevelt Library

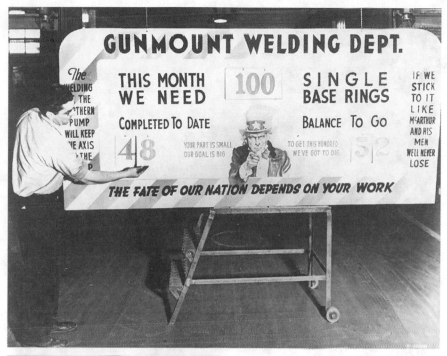

GUNMOUNT WELDING DEPT.

The WELDING OF THE NORTHERN PUMP WILL KEEP THE AXIS THE P

THIS MONTH WE NEED **100** SINGLE BASE RINGS

IF WE STICK TO IT LIKE M^cARTHUR AND HIS MEN WELL NEVER LOSE

COMPLETED TO DATE

BALANCE TO GO

48

YOUR PART IS SMALL OUR GOAL IS BIG

TO GET THIS HUNDRED WE'VE GOT TO DIG

52

THE FATE OF OUR NATION DEPENDS ON YOUR WORK

UNITED WE WIN

Above: The labor-management committee at the Northern Pump Company used this scoreboard to encourage productivity in 1943. Courtesy Franklin D. Roosevelt Library
Left: Poster encouraging good race relations in the workplace, from the War Manpower Commission.
National Archives NWDNS-44-PA-370

When you ride ALONE
you ride with Hitler!

Join a
Car-Sharing Club
TODAY!

*Above: Experienced assembly line
workers of both sexes contribute
to the production of an A-20 attack
bomber at the Douglas Aircraft
plant in Long Beach, CA.* Courtesy
Franklin D. Roosevelt Library
*Right: Poster aimed
at limiting the use of gasoline.*
National Archives NWDNS-188-PP-42

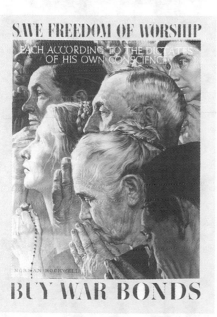

OURS...to fight for

FREEDOM FROM FEAR

SAVE FREEDOM OF SPEECH

BUY WAR BONDS

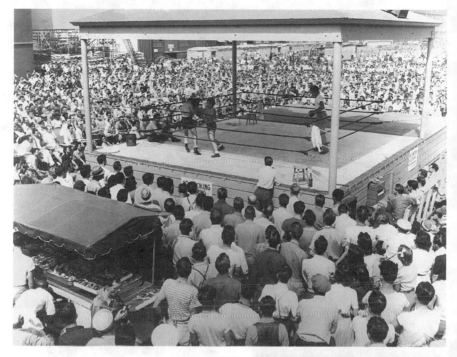

Top: Many recreational programs were offered at North American's Inglewood, CA, plant during lunch periods. Here thousands watch a boxing match between two employees.
Bottom: Two students at Roosevelt High School in Los Angeles take part in Victory Corps activities, one of which encouraged girls to learn to handle firearms, 1942. Courtesy Franklin D. Roosevelt Library

Top: A little girl with scrap
rubber and aluminum for
one of the thousands of
collection drives held
nationwide, 1942.
Bottom: New York City
aluminum collection, 1942.
Courtesy Franklin D. Roosevelt
Library

Top: Sign for an evacuation sale at the Okano Bros. five and dime, as Japanese Americans left San Francisco, 1942. Courtesy Franklin D. Roosevelt Library
Opposite Top: Memorial Day services in 1942, at the War Relocation Authority camp at Manzanar, CA. Courtesy Franklin D. Roosevelt Library
Opposite Bottom: A young Japanese-American boy tagged for evacuation, Salinas, CA, 1942. Library of Congress #LC-USF34T01-72499D

*Top: President Roosevelt,
Philadelphia, 1944.
Bottom: President Roosevelt
with his dog, Fala,
Hyde Park, NY, 1942.*
Courtesy Franklin D.
Roosevelt Library

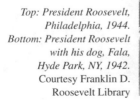

cial reasons or simply refused to abandon what they had gained. That desire came squarely into conflict with the wish of servicemen to return to former positions when they came home, and to resume the patterns of life they remembered from before the war.

Just as industrialists and government officials had campaigned earlier to draw women into war plants, as the war wound down they did an about-face and campaigned to encourage women to be prepared to leave their jobs when the men returned. The federal government emphasized that wartime work was temporary. Betty Allie, a Michigan unemployment official, noted: "When the period of postwar adjustment comes, and their men come home. . . you will see women returning naturally to their homes." Jane Stokes, speaking on the radio for her union in the aircraft industry, declared: "When this war is over—I'll get a manicure, put on the frilliest dress I can find, pour a whole bottle of cologne over my head, and THEN, I'll be GLAD to give up my Union chair in the Eagle Airie Room to some boy who comes marching home deserving it."

As demobilization took place, factories released women at almost double the rate for men. In the summer of 1945, three-fourths of the women in the shipbuilding and aircraft industries were let go; shipbuilding became a male bastion once again. The female share of jobs in the Detroit automobile industry fell from 25 percent to 7.5 percent. Now the positions available to women in all areas were often less attractive and lower paying than those open to men.

While World War II clearly had a powerful effect on women's lives, historians have debated the degree of that impact. William Chafe (*The American Woman*) has underscored the changes that occurred, while subsequent feminist scholars like Susan Hartmann (*The Home Front and Beyond*) and Karen Anderson (*Wartime Women*) have focused instead on the ephemeral nature of wartime changes, arguing that the appeal to women's patriotism led them to work for national ends rather than personal satisfaction, thereby dampening their aspirations once the fighting had ended.

Even though many wartime gains were lost and progress was thwarted in the postwar period, significant changes had occurred in the lives of American women. The struggle had led to improve-

ments in their condition, and the behavioral shifts that took place on the part of both sexes helped foster the groundwork for a women's movement in later years. Indeed, World War II was an important step on the long road to equal rights.

African Americans and the War

World War likewise helped promote the cause of equality for African Americans in the United States. A movement aimed at ending discrimination against blacks had been underway since the early years of the twentieth century, but they remained acutely aware of the gap between the American dream and reality in the United States. In the South, the Jim Crow system, which mandated rigid separation of the races, remained firmly entrenched. Though segregation was less legally binding in the North, residential patterns, with blacks congregated in urban ghettoes and slums, yielded a similarly divided, and unequal society. Organizations such as the National Association for the Advancement of Colored People (NAACP) protested racist conditions and sought to chip away at the framework of segregation, but progress was halting at best.

African Americans had realized only modest changes in their daily lives in the first few decades of the twentieth century. Though they had strongly supported the American effort in World War I, blacks had discovered in its aftermath little inclination on the part of an ungrateful government and public to support them in their ongoing struggle for equal rights. While the New Deal had held out hope for change, African Americans found that the administration's other political priorities came first, and little was done for them as a separate group. The only gains they had realized came from programs that assisted the poor in general.

At the start of World War II, African Americans faced discrimination on a variety of fronts. Eight million Americans remained unemployed, but blacks suffered disproportionately, with their rate of unemployment in 1940 almost twice that for whites. Meanwhile, median family income for blacks was just over one-third of that for whites. African Americans found it difficult to obtain skilled positions and held far more unskilled jobs than whites. Employment opportunities opened to blacks frequently were low-

paying jobs as janitors, bellhops, or garage attendants. In 1940, only 240 of the 100,000 workers in the aircraft industry were black, most of them janitors. And the United States Employment Service continued to accept employers' requests for "whites only," thus perpetuating existing discriminatory patterns.

Black women suffered even more than did black men. In the 1930s, the contraction of the national economy had cut the number of jobs previously available to black women, yet they received few of the New Deal benefits that provided a cushion for other poor Americans. As the depression ended, black women remained the last to be offered better jobs. In 1940, three-fourths of them worked as domestic servants or agricultural employees.

The situation of African Americans in the military services was little better. Blacks initially were not allowed to join the air corps or marine corps. In the navy, they could enlist only in the all-black messmen's branch; in the army, they were segregated from whites and confined to the few regular black units created after the Civil War, with combat units still commanded by whites. Black officers generally were assigned to noncombat units.

Humiliations plagued those African Americans who were permitted to serve their country. Blacks were understandably resentful when the army, like the Red Cross, separated blood plasma according to the donor's race. They were bothered too by the slights they encountered when assigned to training camps or duty stations in the South. Lloyd Brown recalled being turned away from a lunchroom in Salina, Kansas, only to see German prisoners of war being served at the same counter. "This was really happening," he exclaimed. "It was no jive talk. The people of Salina would serve these enemy soldiers and turn away black American G.I.s."

Many Americans denied that such injustices existed. A poll taken in 1942 revealed that six out of ten whites felt that blacks were comfortable with the way things were and deserved no further opportunities. A majority believed that blacks' inferior social status was due to individual shortcomings and not to white resistance to change.

Prejudice was strongest in the South, where members of the South Carolina House of Representatives asserted their "allegiance" to white supremacy as they pledged their lives and their

"sacred honor" to maintain the system. But acceptance of the status quo was strong in other parts of the country as well. In the West and Northeast, whites, when interviewed, voiced their approval of separate schools, separate restaurants, and separate neighborhoods.

Popular attitudes were mirrored within the Roosevelt administration. Secretary of War Stimson had strong views on the question of race. The crusty old Republican viewed blacks as inferior, for they had scored lower than whites on World War I intelligence tests; though the tests measured educational achievement rather than intelligence, Stimson's mind was set: blacks were unfit for advancement. "Leadership," he said, "is not embedded in the negro race yet and to try to make commissioned officers to lead men into battle—colored men—is only to work disaster to both." General George C. Marshall, a Virginian responsible for organizing the massive military effort from Washington, agreed. Desegregation, he felt, would destroy morale by changing patterns "established by the American people through custom and habit."

Roosevelt himself was more concerned with military questions than minority rights. The "integrity of our nation and our war aims is at stake in our attitude toward minority groups at home," he acknowledged, but he was reluctant to engage in long-range future planning. "I don't think, quite frankly," he said at the end of 1943, "that we can bring about the millenium at this time."

Yet a movement for change was underway. Richard M. Dalfiume ("The Forgotten Years of the Negro Revolution," *Journal of American History,* 1968) was one of the first to point to the roots of postwar reform in the war period itself, and Neil A. Wynn (*The Afro-American and the Second World War,* 1976) later provided the fullest and best-documented account of the African-American experience during the war.

Agitation resulted in part from the stark contrast between professed ideals and actual practice in the United States, particularly when engaged in a war against a fascist foe. Now blacks pointed out that Jim Crow restrictions resembled the racist regulations of Nazi Germany. Noting the paradox, one soldier writing to FDR observed that the army, the "very instrument which our government has organized and built . . . to fight for world democracy, is within itself undemocratic."

Pressures to effect change stemmed too from the force of numbers. Like whites, blacks gravitated toward industrial centers in search of work, though the black migration lagged behind the white movement and was, in the end, less massive than the black diaspora during World War I. Still, some 700,000 blacks moved during the Second World War, 400,000 of them leaving the South. Between 1940 and 1946, the black population in San Francisco grew 560 percent, compared to a 28.1 percent white increase. In Los Angeles, black growth was 109 percent compared to 17.7 percent for whites. In Detroit's Willow Run area, black growth was 47 percent compared to 5.2 percent for whites. Concentration only exacerbated and gave voice to common grievances.

Blacks became increasingly assertive and launched a two-pronged attack of their own. The *Pittsburgh Courier*, a widely circulated black newspaper, proclaimed a "Double V" campaign—V for victory in the war against the dictators overseas, V for victory in the struggle for fair treatment at home. Blacks "would be less than men," the *Courier* suggested, "if, while we are giving up our property and sacrificing our lives, we do not agitate, contend, and demand those rights guaranteed to all free men. . . this would be neither patriotism nor common sense." African Americans demanded something more from the war than the wry epitaph that originated during the period: "Here lies a black man killed fighting a yellow man for the protection of a white man."

Forces for change began to coalesce in January 1941, when A. Philip Randolph, head of the Brotherhood of Sleeping Car Porters, proposed a massive March on Washington under the slogan: "WE LOYAL NEGRO AMERICAN CITIZENS DEMAND THE RIGHT TO WORK AND FIGHT FOR OUR COUNTRY." Randolph, as Jervis Anderson (*A. Philip Randolph: A Biographical Portrait,* 1973) has shown, was a firm believer in the use of power. "The Administration leaders in Washington," he declared, "will never give the Negro justice until they see masses—ten, twenty, fifty thousand Negroes on the White House lawn!" He wanted a "thundering march" that would "shake up white America."

The March on Washington Movement sought to exclude whites on the premise that blacks had to fight for their rights on their own. In advocating that blacks work together to attain their

common goals, Randolph wanted to "create faith by Negroes in Negroes." The movement also sought to mobilize the masses rather than the black middle class, and it underscored the need for direct action on an unprecedented scale, as opposed to quiet negotiation and compromise.

When Randolph met with the president in mid-June 1941, he presented a series of demands. He wanted an end to discrimination in employment, an end to discrimination and segregation in the federal government, and an end to discrimination and segregation in the armed forces. Roosevelt was worried about the possibility of violence in Washington, a city with southern values and customs, and had already attempted to head off the march with expressions of support for equal opportunity. Meeting Randolph face-to-face, the president tried to use his well-known powers of persuasion to get him to back off, but the black leader pressed for "something concrete, something tangible." They finally agreed that a committee would draft an executive order, subject to Randolph's approval, to meet his demands.

Accordingly, one week later Roosevelt signed Executive Order 8802, declaring "that there shall be no discrimination in the employment of workers in defense industries or government because of race, creed, color, or national origin." To implement the policy, he created a Fair Employment Practices Committee (FEPC) to investigate complaints and take appropriate action. In response, Randolph called off the march.

Unfortunately, the FEPC was never wholly effective. As Merl E. Reed (*Seedtime for the Modern Civil Rights Movement: The President's Committee on Fair Employment Practice, 1941–1946*, 1991) and Andrew E. Kersten (*Race, Jobs, and the War: The FEPC in the Midwest, 1941–1946*, 2000) have shown, the committee faced obstacles on many fronts. It was underfunded and understaffed from the start. Initially composed of six part-time members and a small staff, it had a budget of a mere $80,000 in its first year. It began operations in the Office of Production Management, moved to the War Production Board, and a year after its creation found itself in the War Manpower Commission. But change of location seldom brought improvement in its ability to fulfill its responsibilities.

The FEPC's powers were severely circumscribed. It was a temporary war agency dealing solely with defense industries. Furthermore, it could only act against discrimination in response to formal complaints, which came relatively infrequently. And even when discrimination was evident and proof forthcoming, the agency lacked the authority to enforce its recommendations. It had to rely on publicity and persuasion to facilitate change. Concerned more with production than promotion of equality, the president remained aloof. But in mid-1943, as manpower needs became more pressing, he moved the FEPC to the Executive Office. Now, with new leadership, a larger budget, and increased authority to conduct investigations, the agency became more aggressive. Chairman Malcolm Ross was aware of both its limitations and possibilities. "We may not be able to wipe out discrimination overnight," he said, "but where war manpower needs are at stake we can and shall try."

The FEPC enjoyed a few notable successes. In the summer of 1944, after it directed that blacks be upgraded to positions as streetcar operators in Philadelphia, a public transportation strike paralyzed the city. With war production jeopardized, the government responded immediately. The army assigned soldiers to mass-transit vehicles to serve as armed guards, the FBI arrested strikers, and the selective service system warned, as it had done in other cases, that it would draft employees who did not return to work. The strike, as Allan M. Winkler ("The Philadelphia Transit Strike of 1944," *Journal of American History,* 1972) has observed, ended in victory for the forces favoring racial equality, but only because the threat to military needs led the government to act.

On balance, the accomplishments of the FEPC were limited. The agency successfully resolved only one-third of the 8,000 complaints it received, and but one-fifth of those coming from the South. Employers or unions ignored or defied 35 of 45 compliance orders issued. Yet, as one War Manpower Commission official noted, the FEPC did keep the issue of fair treatment alive: "It forced people to look, day after day, at this problem of the Negro's economic handicaps."

And improvements did occur, particularly after 1943. When the United States Employment Service ceased honoring requests that specified race and the National Labor Relations Board refused

to certify unions that excluded minority membership, the way was cleared for easier black access to the workforce. Between April 1940 and April 1944, the number of blacks employed rose from 4.4 million to 5.3 million, with most of the gains coming in the latter years. In 1942, black workers constituted 3 percent of all war workers; in 1945, the figure was 8 percent. The federal government itself increased the number of black employees from 60,000 to 200,000.

Black women also made gains. As Jacqueline Jones (*Labor of Love, Labor of Sorrow: Black Women, Work, and the Family, from Slavery to the Present,* 1985) has noted, the war opened up better paying jobs and drew some women away from domestic work. But African-American women had to fight fiercely for whatever new positions they obtained. Maya Angelou became the first black streetcar conductor in San Francisco only by going back to the personnel office time and again with "the frequency of a person on salary" until she got the job she wanted. And black women who did secure industrial jobs often had to work in the dirtiest and most dangerous positions in the plant.

Meanwhile, blacks pressed for change on other fronts. The NAACP and the Urban League continued to work in traditional ways: publicizing grievances, exerting political pressure, and using the courts. Other African Americans, following Randolph's example and recognizing that a degree of militancy was necessary, began to take nonviolent yet direct action in pursuit of racial equality. The Committee of Racial Equality (later the Congress of Racial Equality—CORE) was a biracial organization founded by pacifists in 1942 that began to demonstrate against segregation in a number of cities. In Baltimore, Chicago, Denver, and Detroit, CORE members conducted sit-ins at a number of movie theaters and restaurants and achieved their goal: an end to segregation in those public places.

Their example mobilized black students at Howard University in Washington, D.C. In the spring of 1944, a number of them entered Thompson's, a segregated restaurant located where many black government workers could have enjoyed easy access. Outside, other students picketed with signs reading: "Are you for Hitler's Way or the American Way? Make Up Your Mind" and

"We Die Together. Let's Eat Together." In time, their persistence paid off and helped lead to the easing of segregation in some parts of the capital city.

Agitation also brought change on the military front. African Americans felt that if they could fight alongside whites, according to Richard M. Dalfiume (*Desegregation of the United States Armed Forces: Fighting on Two Fronts, 1939–1953,* 1969), they could expect the rights and privileges of full American citizenship. As the *Crisis,* the publication of the NAACP, declared: "This is no fight merely to wear a uniform. This is a struggle for status, a struggle to take democracy off of parchment and give it life." Black spokesmen pressured legislative and executive leaders even before Pearl Harbor, and their efforts brought the promotion of Colonel Benjamin O. Davis to the rank of general—the first such appointment in American history. They also managed to change policy so that blacks were eligible for general service in the navy and marine corps, though still on a segregated basis. The army air corps eased restrictions too, eventually providing African-American pilots and crews with the chance for combat. Aviators in the black 99th Pursuit Squadron and 332nd Fighter Group (the Tuskegee Airmen) served with distinction. Needing manpower, the army also accepted more and more African Americans, and the number of black soldiers rose from 97,725 in November 1941 to 701,678 in September 1944. The proportion of blacks in the army still lagged behind the proportion in the general population, and the army remained segregated. Some black volunteers, however, did integrate formerly all-white combat units near the end of the war.

Despite modest progress, racial conflicts persisted throughout the war. The migration of Americans of all races into urban centers of war production strained housing and transportation facilities. But blacks found their housing choices severely limited, and therefore gravitated toward ghetto areas that bulged to the breaking point. In areas of San Francisco formerly inhabited by the Japanese, 10,000 people lived where 5,000 had lived before. In Chicago, 300,000 blacks crowded into the South Side in a region thought able to hold a maximum of 225,000 persons.

Detroit too was terribly overcrowded. By 1943, half of the black families there lived in substandard homes. The year before, the city faced a serious struggle over the Sojourner Truth housing project, built for blacks, then demanded by whites who felt overcrowded too. Though African Americans protested this encroachment and eventually won the day, ensuring that the complex remained designated for blacks, the dispute fostered ill feeling on both sides. Tensions were growing more intense all the time. In August 1942, *Life* magazine published a story entitled "Detroit Is Dynamite," and concluded that "Detroit can either blow up Hitler or it can blow up the U.S."

The explosion, described by Harvard Sitkoff in "The Detroit Race Riot of 1943" (*Michigan History,* 1969), came on a Sunday evening in June, in the midst of a heat wave. One hundred thousand people, 85 percent of them black, congregated in Belle Isle, a recreation park near the black ghetto of Paradise Valley. Scuffles between blacks and whites early in the evening led to more serious violence as night fell. Rumors of rape and murder spread. The most common story was that whites had thrown a black woman and her baby off a bridge. Before long, a full-scale race riot was underway. Blacks looted and destroyed white-owned stores. Whites pulled blacks out of theaters and off streetcars and beat them. The police stood by and did little, except shoot some looters. By the time the riot ended several days later, 25 blacks and 9 whites were dead, 675 people were injured, and about $2 million of property was destroyed.

In New York City's Harlem, another uprising, described by Dominic J. Capeci in *The Harlem Riot of 1943* (1977), took place at the beginning of August. When a rumor spread that a policeman had killed a black soldier, the community erupted. Sweeping through the business district, blacks smashed windows, entered stores, and carried away goods. Though no battles between blacks and whites took place, 6 blacks were killed and 300 were injured. The Harlem uprising reflected the same frustrations and resentments that erupted in Detroit and surfaced in other cities throughout the nation.

To what degree did the war bring lasting change for African Americans? Without question, it broke down some societal barri-

ers. Increased access to the military services and to industrial positions made a difference. So did the Supreme Court's decision abolishing the white primary election in 1944. At the same time, such modest gains may, in fact, have had the effect of dampening the nascent civil rights movement's momentum. Though a start toward greater equality had been made, blacks remained disadvantaged, politically, socially, and economically. Black soldiers returning home soon recognized that there was still a long way to go, as one on his way back from the Pacific observed when he declared, *"Our fight for freedom begins when we get to San Francisco."* Further change was necessary, and an explosive force was building that could no longer be contained. As Walter White, head of the NAACP, wrote: "A wind *is* rising—a wind of determination by the havenots of the world to share the benefits of freedom and prosperity which the haves of the world have tried to keep exclusively for themselves. . . . Whether that wind develops into a hurricane is a decision we must make."

Latinos and the War

Like women and African Americans, Latinos faced discrimination during World War II. In 1940, about 1.5 million Spanish-speaking people lived in the United States. Some came from Puerto Rico; others emigrated from Central and South America. Some settled in eastern cities; many more lived in the West and Southwest. Chicanos—Mexican Americans—were the most numerous of all. Invisible in the first treatments of World War II, Latinos have begun to receive more attention in monographs and history texts in recent years. Rodolfo Acuña (*Occupied America: A History of Chicanos,* 3rd edition, 1988) provided the first comprehensive overview of Chicanos, including an account of their activities during the war. More recently, George J. Sánchez (*Becoming Mexican American: Ethnicity, Culture and Identity in Chicano Los Angeles, 1900–1945,* 1993) and Ronald Takaki (A *Different Mirror: A History of Multicultural America* (1993) have examined the difficulties Latinos encountered and the contributions they made in wartime.

During the struggle, Chicanos faced both racial and ethnic discrimination, often segregated along with blacks on the basis of skin color. At the same time, they had to deal with the additional disadvantage of speaking a foreign language. "For Coloreds and Mexicans," a characteristic sign outside a Texas church read. Often deprived of adequate jobs, they tended to settle in run-down areas. Lacking political influence, they found it difficult to break the poverty cycle.

Alfred Barela, a Mexican-American youth, eloquently summed up Latino frustrations in May 1943, when charged with disturbing the peace. In a letter to the municipal judge, he wrote:

Ever since I can remember I've been pushed around and called names because I'm a Mexican. I was born in this country. Like you said I have the same rights and privileges as other Americans. . . . Pretty soon I guess I'll be in the army and I'll be glad to go. But I want to be treated like everybody else. We're tired of being pushed around. We're tired of being told we can't go to this show or that dance hall because we're Mexican or that we better not be seen on the beach front, or that we can't wear draped pants or have our hair cut the way we want to. . . . I don't want any more trouble and I don't want anyone saying my people are in disgrace. My people work hard, fight hard in the army and navy of the United States. They're good Americans and they should have justice.

The discrimination and frustration notwithstanding, wartime manpower shortages helped Chicanos just as they helped other groups. When military personnel were needed, the government drafted 350,000 Mexican Americans into the armed forces, and eventually half a million Mexican Americans served in the military. Some were members of the 200th and 515th Coast Artillery units of the New Mexico National Guard, already in the Philippines (because they spoke Spanish) before the Japanese attack on Pearl Harbor. Many of the Chicano soldiers paid a heavy price. Congressman Jerry Voorhis of California observed: "As I read the casualty lists from my state, I find anywhere from one-fourth to one-third of those names are names such as Gonzalez or Sanchez, names indicating that the very lifeblood of our citizens of Latin-American descent in the uniform of the armed forces of the United States is being poured out to win victory in the war." While Mexi-

can Americans constituted only 10 percent of the population of Los Angeles, they represented 20 percent of the city's casualties, in a pattern true of other areas as well.

Mexican-American farm workers, like other rural Americans, gravitated to the cities in search of better jobs, in a trend that had begun in the 1920s. The wartime migration brought significant changes in what had been a largely unskilled, agricultural labor force. Anticipating future manpower needs, between 1939 and 1942 the Department of Labor's Office of Education established vocational schools in cities such as Albuquerque and Sante Fe, New Mexico, and Las Vegas, Nevada. The schools provided rural arrivals with training as plumbers, mechanics, and welders, and eased the transition into war work.

Chicanos made striking gains. In 1941, no Mexican American was employed in the Los Angeles shipyards; by 1944, 17,000 Chicanos worked there. They also worked in shipyards and aircraft factories in Seattle, Long Beach, Corpus Christi and Albuquerque. Some headed for other major war production cities, such as Detroit, Chicago, Kansas City, and New York.

At the same time, changes in agricultural hiring took place. When the war caused an acute farm labor shortage, the United States looked to Mexico for aid. Faced with the problem of providing food for both the home front and the military, American growers sought to bring Mexican citizens across the border to work in their fields. Initially, the growers wanted simply to open the border and hire workers at the lowest possible rate, but they were forced to capitulate to rules laid out by a government program when Mexico insisted on contracts guaranteeing the day-laborers basic rights. An agreement in 1942 providing for transportation, food, shelter, and medical care for the workers led to the entrance of several hundred thousand *braceros* (translated as "helping arms") over the next few years. They worked in a total of 21 states, and in 1944 alone these workers harvested crops worth $432 million. The braceros helped grow and harvest peaches, plums, tomatoes, sugar beets, and cotton, and they worked on railroads as well.

Despite protective agreements and new jobs, Mexicans and Mexican Americans continued to suffer discrimination in the Uni-

ted States. Braceros grumbled about withheld wages and miserable working conditions. Industrial employees often were passed over when available supervisory or skilled jobs went to whites. And they sometimes received lower wages for the same work as that done by white males.

Chicano discontent, like black frustration, was most palpable in the crowded cities. Some young Mexican Americans, uncomfortable in white society, roamed the streets in groups or gangs. Known as *pachucos,* these youths favored a distinctive style of dress—the zoot suit—consisting of trousers flared at the knees but tighter at the ankles, a loosely cut coat reaching to mid-thigh, a long key chain, and a felt hat. Such an outfit set the wearer apart and frightened middle-class Americans, who associated the zoot suit with gang activity and violence.

The atmosphere in Los Angeles, where many Chicanos lived, was volatile. Newspapers abetted white fears by claiming there was a marked increase in crime attributable to the city's Mexican residents. Soon a city council ordinance prohibited the wearing of zoot suits. Police units roamed through East Los Angeles and made spot searches, usually without cause. Then, in August 1942, a young Mexican was found lying on a dirt road near the Sleepy Lagoon just outside the city; he died without regaining consciousness. Charging foul play, the police used the corpse as an excuse to round up 22 Mexican-American gang members and beat confessions out of them. Two of the men requested a separate trial and retained competent legal counsel, which resulted in the dropping of the charges against them. But in a travesty of justice only later reversed, 12 of the other defendants were convicted of murder, 5 of them were convicted of manslaughter, and 3 of them were placed on probation.

An even worse episode occurred in early June 1943, when a group of sailors based in Los Angeles sought revenge on a group of Chicanos who had allegedly attacked them during a night on the town. Rampaging through the streets, the sailors stormed into bars and movie theaters, seizing pachucos and tearing zoot suits from their bodies. Innocent people were engulfed in the violence. Pedro García, a native-born American high school senior about to graduate, was sitting in a theater enjoying a film when servicemen burst

in, grabbed him, and dragged him out into the street. Ripping off his clothes, they kicked him, beat him, and left him bloody and unconscious. In this episode and others, both military and civilian law enforcement officials either stood aside or arrested Chicanos without cause as the press fanned the flames of racial tension. Eventually, naval personnel were ordered back to their ships or bases and the riot came to an end, a surge of anger in its wake.

Chicanos hoped the war would help them achieve the equality they sought. As one soldier observed as he went off to fight, "All we wanted was a chance to prove how loyal and American we were." For soldiers and civilians both, the war helped Chicanos move closer to enjoying the rights and benefits of full citizenship. As Manuel De La Raza declared in 1942, "This war. . . is doing what we in our Mexican-American movement had planned to do in one generation. . . . It has shown those 'across the tracks' that we all share the same problems. It has shown them what the Mexican Americans will do, what responsibility he will take and what leadership qualities he will demonstrate. After this struggle, the status of the Mexican Americans will be different."

American Indians and the War

American Indians in the United States also became actively involved in the war effort. Like African Americans and Latinos, the 345,000 American Indians in 1940 had long been regarded as second-class citizens, and they were still denied the right to vote in several states. This pattern of extended mistreatment over a period of 150 years, Commissioner of Indian Affairs John Collier observed in "The Indian in a Wartime Nation" (*The Annals of the American Academy of Political and Social Science,* 1942), "could hardly be expected to produce loyal citizens devoted to the Nation's welfare and willing to defend it against its enemies." Yet Indians, like members of other minority groups, sensed the larger stakes of the struggle and willingly offered their support to the nation's military and industrial sectors.

During the war, approximately 25,000 served in all branches of the military, most of them in the army. Some were drafted; others volunteered. Indians from tribes with a warrior tradition

proved especially willing to enlist. The Mission Indian Federation of California sent "a message of loyalty and readiness to serve our great Nation." The Crow tribe of Montana enthusiastically offered the government all of its eligible manpower.

Indians served ably in combat and in providing military support. Ira Hayes, a Pima from Arizona, received extensive media coverage as one of three survivors at Mount Suribachi on Iwo Jima where Marines, after fighting a heroic and legendary battle, managed to raise the American flag. Some Navajos worked as code talkers. Their language was so rare that it served as a secret means for transmitting marine corps messages by radio and phone, particularly in the Pacific campaigns. Lacking an alphabet and relying on a complicated syntax, the language served as a cryptic but reliable way of slipping sensitive orders and commands through enemy lines.

Still, Indians in military service, like other minorities, met with discrimination. Some were relegated to clerical duty or various kinds of menial work. Most suffered from the persistent stereotypes that remained part of American life. Where there was only one Indian in a unit, for example, that man often found himself called "Chief." Nonetheless, military service for the most part went smoothly and many Indians were decorated for their heroic deeds.

Indians made a substantial home-front contribution as well. Approximately 40,000 worked in war industries throughout the country. Two thousand Navajos helped build a sizable ordnance depot in New Mexico. Other Indians constructed aircraft on the West Coast and helped produce all kinds of military materials in major war production centers in other areas.

The war hastened the slow but ongoing process of detribalization, thus accelerating American Indian assimilation into the larger society. As thousands of Indians left their reservations for military or industrial jobs, they had to make rapid adjustments to mainstream American life. When the war ended, some Indians returned to reservations, but many others had been changed by the experience and now were reluctant to settle back into old patterns. Often the process of transition was marked by a sense of alienation and rootlessness, one that became even more pronounced in

the 1950s when the federal government moved toward termination of the reservation system altogether.

World War II had a powerful impact on America's Indian population. It reduced the cultural and physical isolation of many Indians from mainstream society and helped create a mood of greater assertiveness that provided the framework for militancy in later years. The National Congress of American Indians, established in 1944, was a precursor to even more aggressive civil rights organizations in the decades that followed. The war clearly was, as Alison R. Bernstein has argued in *American Indians and World War II: Toward a New Era in Indian Affairs* (1991), the most important event in twentieth-century American Indian history.

Italian Americans under Attack

Some ethnic groups had especially severe problems that were unique to the World War II years. Those who came from nations with which the United States was fighting had the worst time. German Americans, treated poorly by their fellow Americans during the First World War, were now more fully assimilated into American life and were largely left alone. This time Italians and Japanese bore the brunt of the majority's transferred anger.

For Italian Americans, conditions in the United States were often grim. More recently arrived than other European immigrants, most of the nearly 5 million Italians living in the United States were first- or second-generation Americans. In 1942, 600,000 Italian immigrants still were not naturalized, though many who were still aliens had applied for citizenship. Uneducated and unskilled, many of them had trouble finding a decent job. Unassimilated, they felt like outsiders in their new land. Many Italian immigrants, John P. Diggins has argued in *Mussolini and Fascism: The View from America* (1972), looked with pride and affection on Benito Mussolini and the "New Italy." As Paul Pisicano, a resident of an Italian-speaking neighborhood during the war, later recalled, "Mussolini was a hero, a superhero. He made us feel special, especially the southerners, Sicilian, Calabrian."

Italian Americans, caught between two cultures, had lived in an uneasy peace in the prewar years. In June 1940, Franklin Roosevelt aroused their apprehension when he condemned Mussolini for his "stab in the back" of France. A wave of suspicion swept the country, and anti-Italian sentiment became more pronounced than ever before. An executive order the day after Pearl Harbor designated noncitizen Italians as *enemy* aliens. Those so designated, in addition to being hurt and frightened by the decree, now found their physical movement and employment opportunities restricted.

Stung by the stigma and resentful at what they felt was unfair discrimination, Italian Americans worked to have the designation changed. They finally succeeded on Columbus Day, in October 1942, when the government reversed its policy in formal recognition of the loyalty Italian Americans had shown. Now naturalization procedures were simplified. Highly visible Italian Americans such as baseball player Joe DiMaggio were hailed as the new heroes. The assimilation of this group into American society was finally underway.

Japanese Americans: Civilian Casualties of War

Japanese Americans were far less fortunate than other American ethnic groups. While in the first postwar years a few historians documented the travesties this group suffered, the best accounts of what had occurred emerged later. In *Concentration Camps U.S.A.: Japanese Americans and World War II* (1971), Roger Daniels provided a vivid description of the difficulties Japanese Americans encountered, and he has supplemented that work in a number of other books, most notably *Prisoners Without Trial: Japanese Americans in World War II* (1993). Looking closely at legal issues, Peter Irons, in *Justice at War* (1983), has dissected the Justice Department's decision-making process, which, combined with other factors, led to the forced relocation—and internment—of the Japanese, most of whom were United States citizens. The government's claim that it had to act as it did on military grounds has now been thoroughly debunked in the literature about this disgraceful affair.

Japanese Americans suffered for being a tiny minority who just happened to have come from a nation with which the United States was at war. Though only 127,000 Japanese—roughly one-tenth of 1 percent of the American population—lived in America at the start of the war, they were highly visible and vulnerable. The total population of Japanese Americans comprised some 47,000 *Issei,* first-generation immigrants (born abroad)—who were ineligible for naturalization by the Immigration Act of 1924—and roughly 80,000 *Nisei,* second-generation Japanese Americans (native-born), and their children, *Sansei.* When the war began, most Japanese Americans were concentrated on the West Coast, where racial and ethnic prejudice against Asians had existed since the nineteenth century. The attack on Pearl Harbor gave nativist groups, which had long sought Japanese exclusion, an opportunity to strike. As one Native Son of the Golden West declared, "This is our time to get things done that we have been trying to get done for a quarter of a century."

Anti-Japanese sentiment intensified in the early months of the war. Shocked by what had happened at Pearl Harbor, Americans were prepared to believe the worst and acted accordingly. They saw hostile signs everywhere. Rumors, all of them unfounded, spread about West Coast sabotage. A barbershop in California offered "free shaves for Japs," adding that it was "not responsible for accidents." *Time* and *Life* magazines informed readers how to tell friendly Chinese from enemy Japanese: "The Chinese expression is likely to be more placid, kindly, open; the Japanese more positive, dogmatic, arrogant." There were other differences, too: "Japanese walk stiffly erect. . . Chinese more relaxed. . . sometimes shuffle." Government officials contributed to the attacks on Japanese living in the United States. "A Jap's a Jap," said General John DeWitt, head of the Western Defense Command. "It makes no difference whether he is an American citizen or not. . . . I don't want any of them." The governor of Idaho was even more explicit. "A good solution to the Jap problem would be to send them all back to Japan, then sink the island," he said. "They live like rats, breed like rats, and act like rats." Even liberal journalist Walter Lippmann added his voice to those favoring internment.

Faced with growing political and public pressure, the army cited military necessity to justify its decision to evacuate all West Coast Japanese from their homes. Executive Order 9066, signed by the president in mid-February 1942, referred to all enemy aliens, but was applied only to the Japanese—citizens and noncitizens alike. When evacuation began and it became clear that other parts of the country were unwilling to accept the Japanese internees, the army shifted course. A newly created War Relocation Authority (WRA), acting with presidential and congressional approval, brushed constitutional niceties aside and forcibly moved 110,000 Japanese Americans to ten detention camps in seven western states. Milton Eisenhower, General Dwight D. Eisenhower's brother, served as first head of the agency. He hoped the camps could perform useful projects and thereby transform the mood of the country from bitterness to tolerance toward the Japanese, but he soon realized the naivete of that hope. The populace's hatred for Japanese Americans persisted through the end of the war.

The camps, located in desolate areas far from any coast, ringed by barbed wire, and filled with armed guards, contained shoddy wooden barracks covered by tarpaper and divided into one-room apartments. One camp, in the eastern Sierras in Califonia, has been particularly well described by John Armor and Peter Wright in *Manzanar* (1988). The book features photographs the world-renowned photographer Ansel Adams took in 1943 and a commentary by novelist John Hersey. Manzanar consisted of 504 barracks. Each family of four lived in a space of 20 by 25 feet. Amenities included steel-framed army cots covered by straw mattresses and bare light bulbs hanging from the ceiling. Toilet, laundry, dining, and bathing facilities were communal. Families were referred to by numbers rather than names. In those cramped and stark quarters, traditional familial relationships broke down. Older Japanese found their authority questioned by the younger Nisei who could better handle the daily hardships. Social cohesion disintegrated. "I lost my identity," one woman said. "I lost my privacy and dignity." Some Japanese became seriously depressed. The whole experience, from the time they were first herded off to the camps to the final days of internment, was humiliating and left deep scars.

By 1943, the WRA developed a system of removing those Japanese from the camps who showed no evidence of disloyalty and could perform useful jobs elsewhere in the nation. By the end of 1944, the agency had allowed 35,000 internees, mostly Nisei, to leave. Trouble arose, however, when the War Department tried to register evacuees for military service, and 28 percent of the still-incarcerated male Nisei, feeling that military service should not be their only right of American citizenship and deeply hurt by a government that had betrayed them, protested by refusing to renounce their allegiance to the emperor of Japan. The government's response was to segregate further 18,500 "disloyal" Japanese in another camp in Tule Lake, California—quarters even worse than those in the original camps.

Finally, in early 1945, the administration decided that all the detainees were free to—and must—leave the camps. Some, who had found their only security in the strained quarters and had no homes or property left, were reluctant to go but, once again, had no choice. At first, they received some government assistance in relocating, but soon the WRA left them entirely on their own.

The entire episode was the worst violation of civil liberties in wartime America. In addition to psychological trauma, the Japanese suffered $400 million in income and property losses. Yet the U.S. Supreme Court upheld the evacuation of the Japanese in several court cases in 1944. Only years later was there a measure of recompense. In 1980, Congress established a Commission on Wartime Relocation and Internment of Civilians to review what had been done and to recommend appropriate remedies. After several bills died over the next few years, a law was finally passed in 1988 providing modest financial compensation for the 60,000 surviving internees, and a terrible chapter in the nation's history came to an end.

American Jews and the War

American Jews faced a dilemma during the war. As the horrors of the Holocaust—in which the Nazis murdered some 6 million Jews—were unfolding, the lingering legacy of anti-Semitism in the United States hampered American efforts to help Jews fac-

ing liquidation in Europe. Jews in the United States were aware of the slaughter of their relatives overseas but unable to do anything to help stop the monumental tragedy. At the same time, the Holocaust woke many Americans up to the danger of anti-Semitism and helped promote greater assimilation of Jews into American society.

Jews played an important part in the war. Many of the refugee scientists who helped create the atomic bomb were Jews who had fled Europe as Hitler's intentions became clear. Others worked on different research projects. Millions fought in military units, worked in factories, and staffed offices in the growing bureaucracy. Though some centuries-old stereotypes of the Jew as sly and selfish profiteer persisted and some Jews continued to face prejudice, their active participation in the war helped erode discriminatory quotas that had kept many Jews out of the nation's best schools and companies in years past.

Still, Jews reading reports about the atrocities being committed in Europe felt stymied. As David S. Wyman (*Paper Walls: America and the Refugee Crisis, 1938–1941*, 1968) and Henry L. Feingold (*The Politics of Rescue: The Roosevelt Administration and the Holocaust, 1938–1945*, 1970) have shown, the State Department proved unwilling to help save Jews who might have escaped the death camps because of the obstructionist tactics of the anti-Semitic Assistant Secretary of State Breckinridge Long, who systematically resisted easing rigid and restrictive immigration quotas or otherwise allowing people facing certain death to enter the United States. While the United States accepted more refugees than other nations—perhaps as many as 150,000 by 1942—it had the ability to accept many more. In a sequel account, *The Abandonment of the Jews: America and the Holocaust, 1941–1945,* published in 1984, Wyman concluded that several hundred thousand more Jews could have been saved if American policymakers had seized the initiative. Despite receiving authenticated information about the Nazi extermination policy underway, Roosevelt did nothing for 14 months, and eventually acted only in response to domestic political pressures. "Franklin Roosevelt's indifference to so momentous an historical event as the systematic annihila-

tion of European Jewry," Wyman wrote, "emerges as the worst failure of his presidency."

Conclusion

Outsiders fared differently than other Americans in World War II. Some used military and industrial demands to agitate for change and alter the circumstances of their lives. Women and blacks in particular made substantial gains on the labor front that provided the model for future reform. Latinos and American Indians sought to apply the same kind of pressure, but they were less numerous and less organized and enjoyed fewer gains.

Yet Latinos and Indians were still better off than the unassimilated groups who were the real American victims of the war. Just as the refrain "military necessity" helped some citizens, it hurt others, particularly immigrants from enemy nations. As millions of Americans enjoyed better times, others experienced hardships—not of their own making—they could not overcome. American Jews, who were more comfortable than members of these groups, still had to face the horrors of the Holocaust that decimated the Jewish population overseas. But the Japanese Americans faced the greatest trials of all. For this group, clearly one of the most marginal in the United States, the war brought burdens, not benefits, and revealed the limitations of the American dream.

CHAPTER FOUR

The Politics of War

The political sphere grew increasingly contentious during World War II. While solidarity in the struggle against the Axis powers remained intact from beginning to end, there was growing polarization over domestic issues. The political world has always reflected the major issues of the day, and electoral contests have long served to articulate a culture's values and views. This pattern held true during World War II. The major wartime elections—presidential and congressional—revolved around the concerns Americans felt as they responded to military and industrial demands, concerns about wages, prices, and shortages, and the very process of mobilization itself. These elections dramatized the debates about how home-front priorities should be set and revealed the disagreements over the nature of the postwar world. Political maneuvering, an integral part of the governing process, focused on issues that could not be ignored and delineated the boundaries of American society as it dealt with the experience of war.

During the Second World War, the United States became increasingly conservative at home. Republicans and southern Demo-

crats, who had begun to resist what they considered the encroach-
ments of the New Deal even before the start of the war, now found
the way clear to implement the cutbacks they sought. The administration, dependent on bipartisan support for its military initiatives, was unwilling to resist their efforts, particularly given the return of prosperity. Though serious inequities still existed in the
United States, further reform had to wait.

Yet the Roosevelt coalition, created in 1936 (and described in
detail by Samuel Lubell in *The Future of American Politics,* 1951),
remained intact. Composed largely of urban, ethnic members of the
working class, many of them Catholic, along with white southerners, the coalition continued to be a powerful force in American
political life, even as pluralities declined. Although it faced constant challenge and underwent continuous change, it stuck together in the presidential election years. It was less successful,
however, in the midterm contests when FDR was not running for
office himself.

The Elections of 1940 and 1942

Franklin Roosevelt, still the dominant political force after eight years
in the White House, sought an unprecedented third term in 1940. As
the nation was just starting to recover from the depression, it was also
beginning to worry about the European war. The conflict, which began in 1939, gave rise to growing concern the next year as Adolf
Hitler overran western Europe and threatened the rest of the world.
In mid-1940, France fell to the Axis powers while the plight of
Great Britain became more desperate. As Americans began providing more aid to beleaguered allies overseas, they became increasingly aware of the possibility of formal American involvement
in the conflict. Faced with an issue of unprecedented importance,
Roosevelt, who had dreamed of retiring and returning to his home
in Hyde Park, New York, felt he had no choice but to run again.

The Republicans first considered Thomas E. Dewey, the
young district attorney in Manhattan, and Robert A. Taft, the conservative senator from Ohio, as prospective candidates for their
presidential nomination. As the Nazi blitzkrieg swept through Eur-

ope, however, party officials worried that Dewey was too young and Taft too committed to an isolationist policy, so they approached Wendell L. Willkie, a business executive from Indiana. The energetic Willkie was a dark horse who ran a brilliant campaign in pursuit of the nomination. President of the Commonwealth and Southern Utilities Corporation, Willkie had come to believe that the New Deal had gone too far, even though he had voted Democratic most of his life. Willkie had widespread support. *Time, Look,* and other magazines touted him; two thousand Willkie clubs supported him; and at the convention, his supporters chanted "We Want Willkie" even when no business was being conducted. When the balloting began, Willkie's campaign gathered momentum, and on the sixth ballot he won the nomination.

In the general campaign, the Republicans criticized the centralizing tendencies of the New Deal and condemned its inability to achieve recovery. The New Deal threatened individualism and free enterprise, Willkie charged, and destroyed private initiative. "Only the productive can be strong," he declared throughout the campaign, and "only the strong can be free." Though Willkie at first supported the administration's foreign policy initiatives, he claimed that the harassment and restriction of business had undermined defense efforts and left the nation unable to protect itself. Roosevelt countered by pointing to defense preparations already underway and to the economic dividends those efforts were paying by putting people back to work. Inspection tours of defense plants and military installations drew attention to the positive results.

As he continued to trail the president in the polls, Willkie sharpened his attack. Seizing upon Americanism as an issue, he charged that dictatorship was possible if Roosevelt gained a third term. Another victory for FDR, he alleged, would violate a sacred principle of American government and lead to a totalitarian end. Willkie also shifted course on the issue of defense. Eager to gain the support of his party's isolationist wing, he now argued that Roosevelt intended to lead the nation into war.

Roosevelt responded in a series of blistering speeches aimed at convincing anxious Americans of his dedication to peace. He sought to reassure ethnic groups like the Irish, Italians, and Germans of his commitment to neutrality, particularly when they wor-

ried that the United States might indeed enter the war and voiced fears about the consequences they might face should the nation align itself with the British against the Axis nations. Underscoring his intention of keeping the nation out of war, Roosevelt proclaimed: "I have said this before, but I shall say it again and again and again: Your boys are not going to be sent into any foreign wars." When it was pointed out that the nation might be attacked and that he might not be able to keep his promise, the president retorted that in case of attack it would no longer be a foreign war.

As election day approached, the campaign became even nastier. The Democratic vice presidential candidate, Henry A. Wallace, came close to suggesting that a vote for Willkie was a vote for Hitler. But as Willkie's rhetoric intensified, so did attacks on him. Wherever he went he faced a barrage of eggs, rocks, and other objects, along with loud booing. The *New York Times* ran a daily box score of the number of objects hurled at him and targets hit.

In the end, the election turned on FDR. Though his opponents still cringed at the thought of "that man," after two terms in office Roosevelt remained overwhelmingly popular with laborers and other low-income voters, who credited him with the return of prosperity that they already were beginning to perceive. Roosevelt won 55 percent of the popular vote and gained a 334 to 197 vote victory in the electoral college. His 5 million vote margin was considerably smaller than his 11 million vote plurality in the 1936 election, but it was still enough for a clear-cut win. Once again, as John W. Jeffries has demonstrated in his sophisticated quantitative analysis, *Testing the Roosevelt Coalition: Connecticut Society and Politics in the Era of World War II* (1979), FDR's strength came in the cities from foreign-stock, working-class groups who kept the New Deal coalition alive. He won, Jeffries has noted in *Wartime America,* nearly four-fifths of the lower-income vote, three-fifths of the middle income vote, and two-fifths of the upper income vote. In the 1940 congressional contests, the Democrats gained slightly in the House but the Republicans picked up five seats in the Senate. Still, the Democratic party retained control of both chambers with sizable majorities. In the final analysis, the election deepened the political currents of the 1930s and made them a permanent part of American life.

The Democrats had a tougher time in 1942. In the midterm elections, they confronted a growing conservative coalition that really came into its own during the war and played a major role in the politics of the period. This opposition group had been forming for the past five years. According to James T. Patterson (*Congressional Conservatism and the New Deal: The Growth of the Conservative Coalition in Congress 1933–1939,* 1967), it had began to coalesce as early as 1937, when rural elements of FDR's constituency had objected to proposals aimed at assisting northern industrial groups. The president's effort to pack the Supreme Court after his victory in the election of 1936 had provided his opponents with a ready-made issue, and from that time on Republicans and southern Democrats banded together to resist as many of FDR's liberal programs as they could. In the early 1940s, this conservative coalition blocked administration initiatives on all but war-related questions.

In that political setting, the war intensified the resistance of different groups to Roosevelt. Farmers favoring high food prices grumbled about price controls aimed at checking inflation for consumers around the country. Southerners complained when worker shortages extended greater employment opportunities to blacks and talked of bolting the Democratic party. Republicans pointed to inefficiency in the war mobilization effort and to the adverse effects of mobilization on constituent groups. While "Congress cannot assume to run the war," Republican Senator Robert A. Taft acknowledged, "it does have the job of reasonable criticism." Taft and his colleagues were intent on making sure that their voices were heard and their wishes heeded on the home front.

The resistance became clearly visible in 1942, when people who were prosperous once more could afford to forget the assistance the Democrats had given them in the past. With the war proceeding poorly on the military front, there seemed to be cause for complaint.

Republicans made substantial gains in the 1942 congressional elections. They won an additional 44 seats in the House, giving them a total of 209—only 13 fewer than the Democrats' 222—and 9 more seats in the Senate. Low voter turnout made a significant

difference in the final results; only 28 million people voted in 1942, compared to 50 million in 1940. Republican turnout remained relatively stable. The Democratic party—comprising far more draft-age voters, and relocated war workers who had not yet met residency requirements—suffered most of all.

The Republicans knew what they wanted as the new Congress convened. As *Fortune* magazine observed:

The victorious candidates rode an anti-Roosevelt and an anti-Washington wave. They were almost entirely normalcy men, quiet, churchgoing, family men, not quite prohibitionists, men whose outlook was limited to their states and their regions. They may be relied upon to investigate Washington thoroughly. Many of them think they have a mandate to repeal all New Deal reforms.

Compounding the effect of the Republican gains was the increased strength of Democrats from the South. Democratic defeats in the North and Midwest enhanced southern influence in Congress. In the House, representatives from 15 southern and border states claimed 120 of the 222 Democratic seats; in the Senate they held 29 of 57 seats. They also dominated the major committees. When Republicans and southern Democrats banded together, they constituted an almost insurmountable bloc.

The Election of 1944

Despite the 1942 congressional challenge, the president remained politically strong two years later. Physically, however, he had deteriorated. An attack of influenza at the end of 1943 left him debilitated and weak. A general physical examination several months later revealed, according to his personal physician, that FDR suffered from "hypertension, hypertensive heart disease, [and] cardiac failure (left ventricular)." He found his braces—necessary to support his polio-crippled legs—increasingly difficult to use, and he often appeared irritable and worn out.

Nonetheless, Roosevelt was determined to seek another term, and his renomination was never in question. Given the president's failing health, the compelling issue for the Democratic party was

the selection of a vice-presidential nominee. According to John Morton Blum (*The Price of Vision: The Diary of Henry A. Wallace, 1942–1946,* 1973), Henry A. Wallace, FDR's choice in 1940, had drifted beyond the shifting consensus of American politics. The idealistic Wallace had asserted his commitment to internationalism vigorously, but it was an internationalism defined in different terms than those of some Americans. When *Life* magazine publisher Henry Luce proclaimed "the American Century"—where American might would be predominant throughout the globe—Wallace countered that "the century on which we are entering—the century which will come out of this war—can and must be the century of the common man." Even more problematical, he remained committed to the course of domestic reform at a time when other Americans, or at least their representatives in Congress, were willing to pause or turn back.

Roosevelt could have tried to dictate his choice of a running mate as he had in 1940. Instead, bowing to political realities, he left the selection to the convention itself. There, after a behind-the-scenes struggle that included Alben Barkley, Senate majority leader from Kentucky, William O. Douglas, a New Dealer now on the Supreme Court, and James F. Byrnes, Roosevelt's "assistant president" in charge of mobilization, Harry S Truman, senator from Missouri, emerged with the nomination. Truman was a compromise choice, acceptable to all. His Missouri background reassured the South; his ties to the notorious Pendergast machine that dominated the state made political bosses sympathetic; and his leadership of a Senate committee that investigated the defense program gave him liberal support.

On the Republican front, Thomas E. Dewey, now governor of New York, was the leading candidate. After making his reputation by prosecuting underworld figures, Dewey had forged an impressive record as governor. Although he had revamped the state's fiscal system, improved the workmen's compensation system, and arranged for low-income housing subsidies—all reform measures—he argued that the New Deal had gone too far. "It is absolutely necessary that we get rid of the New Deal to save the country," he declared in 1940.

Dewey won the nomination this time, but his age and personality were liabilities that did not endear him to the electorate. At 42, he still seemed too young to be president. Moreover, he appeared arrogant, stiff, and dull. "How can we be expected to vote for a man who looks like the bridegroom on a wedding cake?" Alice Roosevelt Longworth, Theodore Roosevelt's daughter, asked. "Smile, Governor," a photographer once said. "I thought I was," Dewey replied. Critics claimed he suffered from "intellectual halitosis," and declared he was a man "who could strut sitting down."

In the 1944 campaign, both candidates responded to voters' desires for postwar prosperity and peace. Both endorsed some kind of international organization that could help promote future stability as internationalism came of age, and both tried to provide assurance of domestic stability in the years ahead. The possibility of postwar unemployment was a pressing public concern. The war had brought an end to the trials of the Great Depression. Would the nation revert back to pre-1940 conditions once the struggle was over? In industrial states like Connecticut, where nine out of ten workers were engaged in war production, unemployment fears were particularly pronounced. Roosevelt and Dewey agreed that the government had a responsibility to guarantee the availability of jobs.

Disagreements surfaced in other areas. The Democrats took advantage of their close ties with labor. Hoping for a large working-class turnout, since two out of three union members called themselves Democrats, Roosevelt forces launched massive drives to register new voters. A thousand Democratic workers canvassed Detroit; in St. Louis, their counterparts registered 36,000 people in a single day. The AFL and CIO cooperated in working for FDR, and the CIO established a Political Action Committee (PAC) to promote Democratic candidates who were sympathetic to labor. The PAC gave organized labor a measure of political clout that Congress had tried to curtail in the Smith-Connally Act of 1943, and through it the CIO raised money, distributed literature, and made sure voters got to the polls. The basic approach was traditional, but the scale of operation was new.

The Republican campaign, which proved dull at the start, soon became venomous. Once again, the Republicans used the Americanism issue, as Willkie had done, but this time they went far beyond the accusations they leveled in 1940. Now they seized on the menace of communism, which they tied to the Democrats and FDR. "Insidious and ominous are the forces of Communism linked with irreligion that are worming their way into our national life," declared vice-presidential nominee John Bricker. "These forces are attempting to take a strangle hold on our nation through the control of the New Deal." Republicans pointed to the alleged communist sympathies of Sidney Hillman, leader of the CIO Political Action Committee, and claimed that Roosevelt had told Democrats to "clear everything with Sidney." PAC really stood for "Party of American Communism," said Clare Booth Luce in her campaign for reelection to Congress from Connecticut.

Republicans also engaged in personal attacks on FDR. Dewey himself called the president "old and tired." Others circulated rumors about Roosevelt's health and charged that he was dying of diseases ranging from cancer to syphilis. Newspaperman Drew Pearson accused the president of sending a navy destroyer back to the Aleutian Islands, at taxpayers' expense, to retrieve his little dog, Fala, who had been left behind.

FDR fought back. The campaign, described vividly by James MacGregor Burns (*Roosevelt: The Soldier of Freedom*, 1970), seemed to revive and reanimate FDR. At a banquet given by labor officials in September, he deftly demonstrated that he had lost none of his political punch. In his speech, broadcast nationwide over radio, he disposed of the health issue with the acknowledgment that since the last campaign, "I am actually four years older, which is a fact that seems to an-*noy some* people." As he defended his record and challenged the Republicans, his deadpan delivery and mock seriousness brought laughs and cheers. And then he came to the question of his dog: "These Republican leaders have not been content with attacks—on me, or my wife, or on my sons. No, not content with that, they now include my little dog, Fala. Well, of course, I don't resent attacks, and my family doesn't resent attacks, but Fala *does* resent them. I am accustomed to hearing malicious falsehoods about myself—such as that old,

worm-eaten chestnut that I have represented myself as indispensable," he went on. "But I think I have a right to resent, to object to libelous statements about my dog."

In the balloting, Roosevelt won again. His plurality—3.6 million votes—and his share of the popular vote—53.4 percent—both were down from 1940, but he still emerged with an overwhelming 432 to 99 vote victory in the electoral college. Once again, the urban vote made the difference. In cities larger than 100,000, Roosevelt received nearly 61 percent of the vote. He won a number of states—New York, New Jersey, and Pennsylvania, among others—because his plurality in the largest city was greater than the Republican majority in other parts of the state. In 1944, the Democratic coalition remained intact, although with minor modifications. FDR lost some support among white southerners but continued to draw strength from the workers, ethnic Americans, and city dwellers who had elected him in the past.

In the congressional elections, the results were mixed. The Democrats won 22 seats in the House, as the urban vote proved decisive in enabling them to regain Republican seats. In the Senate, the Democrats lost just one seat. In neither chamber did the outcome dramatically alter the Republican–southern Democratic coalition. That conservative coalition proved dominant in the legislative sphere, where it had the power to exert its will on the domestic front from the beginning of the war to the end, presidential victories notwithstanding.

The election of 1944 demonstrated the consistency of voting patterns in the Roosevelt years. As John Jeffries has noted in *Wartime America,* there was less change between 1940 and 1944 than in any elections in the entire Roosevelt-Truman era. In 1944, nine out of ten voters cast their ballots the same way as they had four years before. Once again, this election demonstrated continuities in the political realm.

The Impact of the Conservative Coalition

Roosevelt knew the nature of the opposition and tried to respond accordingly. He understood that the process of domestic reform had run its course in the 1930s. He understood, too, that he had to

makc concessions to the conservative coalition in the interest of support for his military conduct of the war. In a press conference at the end of 1943, he declared that the New Deal had come about when the patient—the United States—was suffering from a grave internal disorder. But then, at Pearl Harbor, the patient had been in a terrible external crash. "Old Dr. New Deal," the president said, "didn't know 'nothing' about legs and arms. He knew a great deal about internal medicine, but nothing about surgery. So he got his partner, who was an orthopedic surgeon, Dr. Win-the-War, to take care of this fellow who had been in this bad accident."

Roosevelt's acknowledgment of political reality made little difference in the outcome of legislative contests. The coalition of Republicans and southern Democrats, strong throughout the war, came into play in four of every ten close Senate votes in 1944. Conservatives, as Richard N. Chapman (*Contours of Public Policy, 1939–1945,* 1981) has shown in a systematic numerical analysis, had both the inclination and the ability to change the domestic agenda in ways they had long sought. "It is no longer feared, it is assumed," Librarian of Congress Archibald MacLeish noted, "that the country is headed back to normalcy, that Harding is just around the corner, that the twenties will repeat themselves."

The conservative coalition left its mark on the home front. Arguing that the New Deal had gone too far and that misguided reform efforts had needlessly interfered with individual initiative in the economic realm, the coalition moved to roll back whatever programs it could. Its members wanted to cut back what they considered the inflated size of government, to circumscribe the power of labor, and to end planning for a strong federal role that they contended went too far. They succeeded in virtually every effort.

The first attacks on the New Deal came in 1942. The Civilian Conservation Corps (CCC) had long been one of the more popular agencies of the 1930s. Concerned with conservation of forest and water resources, the CCC had undertaken a number of noteworthy projects over the course of the last decade that had helped the environment in addition to putting people back to work. But even though the agency participated in the defense effort by training enrollees to read blueprints and perform other tasks useful in the

military, by 1942 its mandate had run its course and its enrollment was in decline. Public opinion no longer supported continuing the program. Roosevelt himself, despite a personal fondness for the CCC, suggested that it might remain useful for boys below draft age "for only very nominal purposes, such as looking after parks, historic places, and forests." Congress was unwilling to go even that far and provided just enough money for the orderly liquidation of the agency.

So it was with the Works Progress Administration (WPA). Work relief had made a real difference in the darkest days of the depression, but conditions had improved. Like the CCC, the WPA faced declining numbers as better jobs became available in the massive war production effort. Two-thirds of those on WPA rolls left in the year following Pearl Harbor. Political opponents, long opposed to the boondoggles they claimed the agency had funded, clamored for its dissolution. WPA supporters remained silent. "I'll bet half the people who were on W.P.A. wouldn't admit that fact if they were asked," one Democrat said. Reading the handwriting on the wall, Roosevelt gave the WPA an "honorable discharge" at the end of 1942. The last relief payment came a few months later.

In 1943, the National Youth Administration (NYA) became another wartime casualty. It had survived the year before because it had provided vocational training in skills useful to the defense industries, and because businessmen, who appreciated the way it brought potential recruits to a central location, had spoken in its defense. But when worker shortages required the hiring of untrained workers, the NYA's purpose was undermined. Now critics had the upper hand. Southerners, who objected to the recruitment and training of black workers, argued for the agency's demise. Education officials, perceiving the NYA as a competitor, charged that its existence was the first step toward federal control of education and advised Congress to "kill this octopus before it kills us." Congress obliged by abolishing the agency.

Congress also killed the National Resources Planning Board (NRPB) in 1943. Engaged in formulating plans and assessing priorities for the postwar period, the NRPB issued several pamphlets in 1942 and 1943 that proposed the expansion of social services

and social security coverage for the needy and impoverished. It also called for public works projects to stimulate the economy when such projects became necessary to achieve full employment. Opponents, who had long frowned on any such planning efforts, resisted those suggestions. This was socialism, the president of the National Association of Manufacturers declared. Falling in line with business again, Congress cut off funding for the NRPB and left it with only enough money to conclude its affairs.

Other agencies suffered a similar fate. The Farm Security Administration, which had helped low-income farmers buy land and machinery and thus produce more, found its budget slashed in 1942 and 1943 and was left with barely enough funds to limp along. The Rural Electrification Administration, a source of keen irritation to private power companies, was cut back as well.

In the current mood, even wartime organizations faced the wrath of Congress. The Office of War Information (OWI), America's propaganda agency, infuriated Republicans who charged that the goal of the agency's Domestic Branch was primarily to obtain a fourth term for FDR. Early in 1943, Senator Rufus C. Holman of Oregon came across the first issue of the OWI publication *Victory,* which contained an article about Roosevelt, featuring a picture of FDR set against a background of the American flag. Holman objected to the story, which characterized the president as a kindly man whose philosophy ran counter to "the toryism of the conservative reactionary." The whole magazine, the senator asserted, was but "window dressing" for another Roosevelt campaign. At budget time, OWI opponents joined forces. Representative John Taber of New York called OWI "a haven of refuge for the derelicts" and Representative Joe Starnes of Alabama termed domestic propaganda "a stench to the nostrils of a democratic people." In the face of those attacks, the Domestic Branch was severely circumscribed.

New reform proposals stood little chance of passage. The 1943 Wagner-Murray-Dingell bill, which would have expanded the social security system by extending coverage and increasing benefits, was defeated. There was also trouble over taxation, as John Morton Blum has shown in detail in *From the Morgenthau Diaries.*

The administration's effort to increase federal expenditures likewise sparked a sharp confrontation between the executive and legislative branches. New revenue was necessary to support the war effort, but these funds sometimes proved difficult to obtain. Though the Treasury Department sought $12 billion for 1943, Roosevelt himself insisted that the request be pared down to $10.5 billion. But with the election of 1944 looming, Congress was unwilling to raise taxes and passed a bill providing only $2 billion, simultaneously making substantial tax concessions to business interests.

Furious at the paltry sum the bill provided and incensed at its inequities, Roosevelt sent an angry veto message to Capitol Hill in February 1944. The measure, he said, was "wholly ineffective" for meeting national needs. With its "undefensible privileges for special groups," he went on, "it is not a tax bill but a tax relief bill providing relief not for the needy but for the greedy."

Congress responded in kind. Democratic majority leader Alben Barkley, a longtime supporter of FDR, voiced his personal irritation at the president and resigned, terming the veto message "a calculated and deliberate assault upon the legislative integrity of every member of Congress." He called on his colleagues to override the veto. They did, by overwhelming margins, and Senate Democrats reelected Barkley leader as well.

This time an intransigent Congress had defeated Roosevelt on two counts. First, the measure was unquestionably inadequate for its intended purposes. Second, it was the first revenue act ever passed over a presidential veto. It was but one more indication of the strength of the conservative coalition in national affairs.

The overall pattern for FDR was defeat after defeat on domestic questions. The president found himself constantly hemmed in either by military demands or by political constraints stemming from congressional unwillingness to support him in anything but the war effort.

So it was with reconversion. The real question as the war neared an end was when civilian production could be resumed. Business leaders were anxious to retool as quickly as they could in order to be ready to supply a market long hungry for scarce goods.

Military leaders objected, asserting that to shift course away from military production at this early date would diminish a sense of urgency at home and compromise home-front morale.

When the Allied advance following the D-Day landings on June 6, 1944 slowed down, Roosevelt recognized that he had little latitude to buck the military. Therefore, he eased out Donald Nelson, head of the War Production Board, who had been clamoring for reconversion. FDR would have preferred to have followed a systematic policy that could have accommodated labor's demands for retraining and placement of discharged workers, but in this affair, as in so many others, the president had no choice but to accept the constraints he faced.

Executive Leadership and Expansion

Though Roosevelt was frequently disappointed at the direction of home-front public policy, he understood that wartime needs took precedence. Committed to victory first and foremost in a two-front war, he needed both military and congressional support for his overseas efforts and thus had to accept compromises on domestic questions. Even so, he did whatever he could to keep a liberal agenda alive.

His efforts had the greatest impact in early 1944. In his State of the Union message, Roosevelt drew on the proposition of the now defunct National Resources Planning Board that the postwar government should guarantee economic as well as political rights and called for enactment of "a *second Bill of Rights* under which a new basis of security and prosperity can be established for all." He sought a commitment to provide useful jobs and adequate wages in addition to decent housing, education, and protection from the ravages of old age, illness, accident, or unemployment. "*All* of these rights spell security," he declared. "And after this war is won," he continued, "we must be *prepared* to move *forward,* in the implementation of these rights, to new goals of happiness and well-being."

The Economic Bill of Rights, rooted in the reforms of the New Deal, had little chance of passage. All the same, it expressed

FDR's hope that his administration's past efforts could be renewed when the war was won as part of the effort Alan Brinkley, in the title of one chapter of *The End of Reform,* has called "planning for full employment." Roosevelt wanted to keep the country looking ahead, whatever the actions of Congress, and he repeated his proposals throughout 1944. "We are not going to turn the clock back!" he said. "We are going forward."

Taking the first step toward implementing his vision, the president proposed extending generous benefits to the one group Congress could not deny—the veterans of the war. He had first suggested the idea in the autumn of 1943, then let it proceed in a form recommended by the American Legion, a politically influential veterans' organization, early the next year. His effort, detailed by Keith Olson in *The G.I. Bill, the Veterans and the Colleges* (1974), was successful in 1944. The Servicemen's Readjustment Act—the G.I. Bill—provided liberal unemployment benefits, gave veterans preference in finding jobs, offered them substantial educational assistance (in the form of tuition payments and supplementary grants to meet living expenses), and guaranteed loans for the purchase of a small business, farm, or home. In short, it underscored the commitment to security and prosperity that was so much a part of the American dream.

And despite the challenges faced, the presidency remained strong. While Congress increasingly asserted its own prerogatives, wartime leadership clearly came from the White House. Roosevelt understood the need to provide direction, and, in response to that need, the office of the presidency enjoyed continued growth. The power of the president had been expanding since the first days of the New Deal. Roosevelt had acted more aggressively than had any of his predecessors in delivering messages, drafting bills, and providing direction as the legislative process unfolded. The proliferation of alphabet agencies—the NRA, PWA, WPA, CCC, and TVA, to mention but a few—was a testament to the ever more active executive role. In 1939, as Richard Polenberg (*Reorganizing Roosevelt's Government: The Controversy over Executive Reorganization, 1936–1939,* 1966) has noted, FDR regularized the changes that had taken place with the creation of the Executive

Office, which included the Bureau of the Budget and other agencies that could assist in providing executive direction. Administrative channels and important agencies were now more firmly under central control. The Executive Office provided the mechanism for later expansion of the executive branch and gave Roosevelt the authority to move as he saw fit.

The war brought even further growth, as the entire federal government expanded exponentially. Between 1940 and 1945, the number of civilian employees rose from 1 million to 3.8 million, with much of this expansion occurring in the executive branch. The president assumed sweeping powers that he delegated to the various war agencies. Under the umbrella of the Office of Emergency Management, a whole series of new agencies attempted to meet the demands of defense and war mobilization. Administrative organization had been makeshift in the past. By the middle of the war, a new structure was in place, and a pattern in which people became accustomed to looking to Washington for answers continued long after the war.

Roosevelt insisted on a position of dominance during the war, and within the areas he perceived as most important, he got his way. Historians and other scholars have become increasingly aware of the extent of the growth of presidential power after disclosures made during the war in Vietnam and the Watergate affair. Arthur M. Schlesinger, Jr., in *The Imperial Presidency* (1973), has shown clearly that much of that growth was rooted in the New Deal and World War II years. As commander-in-chief, Roosevelt took responsibility for making the necessary military decisions and for participating in all diplomatic discussions throughout the war. Yet he was equally insistent on the need to maintain power on important questions at home.

In the autumn of 1942, when Congress seemed tempted to balk at price control legislation, FDR asserted his constitutional position. "In the event that the Congress should fail to act, and act adequately, I shall accept the responsibility, and I will act," he said. "The President has the powers, under the Constitution and under congressional acts, to take measures necessary to avert a disaster which would interfere with the winning of the war." Even former President Herbert Hoover agreed with the general prin-

ciple. "To win total war President Roosevelt must have many dictatorial economic powers," he said. "There must be no hesitation in giving them to him and upholding him in them." Despite charges of dictatorship, FDR got his way on the price control issue.

Roosevelt's aggressive position was not possible in every case, he understood, and Congress had to be accorded latitude in other areas, even if it favored policies he deplored. But FDR was prepared to insist on his leadership rights when in his judgment the war hung in the balance. After the struggle, the balance of power between the executive and legislative branches could be brought back into balance.

The Supreme Court upheld the president's position. It approved price controls and the actions taken to relocate the Japanese Americans. It also rejected cases arising from the seizure of war plants. Clearly, strong executive action was not seriously challenged during the war.

Harry S Truman

Though Franklin Roosevelt was undeniably the dominant American leader in World War II, he failed to see the fighting come to a successful end. On April 12, 1945, the ailments that had been plaguing him finally caught up with him. While relaxing at Warm Springs, Georgia, he suffered a massive cerebral hemorrhage and within minutes was dead.

And so, in the final months of the war, political leadership fell to another man, Harry Truman. Little known outside the Senate, Truman now tried to step into Roosevelt's shoes. It was an awesome task. "Who the hell is Harry Truman?" Admiral William D. Leahy had asked when informed the year before of the choice of the vice-presidential nominee. Many other Americans wondered the same thing. Those who knew were not always pleased to find the man from Missouri in the White House. "That Throttlebottom Truman," TVA director David Lilienthal called him during the transition.

Truman, best described recently by Alonzo L. Hamby (*Man of the People: A Life of Harry S. Truman,* 1995) and David McCullough (*Truman,* 1992), was not particularly well prepared for his new job.

Roosevelt had never taken him into his confidence, and Truman, as he assumed power, was therefore poorly informed on the major issues he faced. He felt painfully inadequate at the start. "I don't know whether you fellows ever had a load of hay fall on you," he told reporters the day after he became president, "but when they told me yesterday what had happened, I felt like the moon, the stars and all the planets had fallen on me." To a former Senate colleague he admitted, "I'm not big enough. I'm not big enough for this job." David Lilienthal agreed. "The country," he said, "doesn't deserve to be left this way."

Yet Truman soon became more comfortable in his new position. Deep down he was a feisty politician who responded to challenges head-on. Unlike Roosevelt, he was impulsive. He was eager to act and willing to take matters into his own hands. A sign on his White House desk read, "The Buck Stops Here." Under Secretary of State Joseph C. Grew, for one, was delighted with Truman's brisk manner. "When I saw him today," Grew wrote in the month after Truman assumed command, "I had fourteen problems to take up with him and got through them in less than fifteen minutes with a clear directive on every one of them. You can imagine what a joy it is to deal with a man like that." Critics, however, suggested that Truman sometimes made decisions without thinking through all of the implications.

As he suddenly assumed the world's most powerful office, Truman faced a number of major issues that required difficult decisions. Early in his presidency, he had to decide whether and how to use the atomic bomb. Should the plan to use the new weapon when it was ready be followed? If so, how many bombs should be dropped? What should be targeted? As commander-in-chief, it fell to Truman to determine how enemy surrender could best be achieved, and how Allied cooperation could best be maintained. Meanwhile he was responsible for carrying through with the politically volatile domestic agenda inherited from Franklin Roosevelt.

From the moment he took office, Truman was intent on following Roosevelt's lead. As the war drew to an end, his messages asserted the same governmental responsibility for the maintenance

of economic security that FDR had proclaimed. The Fair Deal, foreshadowed in those early days, followed the example of the New Deal. The political difficulties it encountered on the home front were the same ones that had developed during the war.

Conclusion

Politics, as ever, reflected American priorities in World War II. Basic social values surfaced in all the legislative and electoral contests that occurred, and the full spectrum of home-front attitudes colored political debate. Americans longed for peace and prosperity throughout the struggle, though different groups disagreed on the means to achieve these ends. As they defined new boundaries in public affairs, these disagreements caused domestic policy to shift course.

EPILOGUE

Without question, World War II left the United States different than it had been before. Yet the crucial question remains: Just how different had the nation become? Historians throughout the post-war decades have argued about the intensity of the war's impact, even as they have debated the degree to which it was a watershed in the country's course. The debate began in the first treatments of home-front issues written shortly after the war and has continued unabated in subsequent years, revolving around the relative importance of the many changes sparked by the war. While definitive answers remain elusive, the discussion itself provides a starting point in an attempt to understand the ultimate effect of the struggle.

Some historians have stressed the marked change experienced by wartime America. Richard Polenberg, in *War and Society,* Geoffrey Perrett in *Days of Sadness, Years of Triumph,* and James MacGregor Burns, in *Roosevelt: The Soldier of Freedom,* are among those who have underscored the profound and powerful impact of the cataclysmic conflict. While the nation suffered no physical destruction within continental borders, this analysis posits that the American people's all-encompassing involvement in the greatest struggle ever known brought economic, social, and political change to an unprecedented degree.

The war ushered in the Keynesian revolution as it brought a return of prosperity after the dismal Great Depression. The mas-

sive spending that began in 1940 provided the best possible demonstration of the positive steps that could be taken to mitigate the effects of a business cycle that seemed stalled on a downward turn. After mobilization economists agreed that aggressive public policy *could* make a difference. The way was clear for continuing experimentation with fiscal policy to avoid economic crisis in the years ahead.

World War II promoted the growth of big business, as it underscored the military-industrial links that made possible the massive production necessary to triumph in the end. War Department ties with the nation's largest firms were stronger than ever when the war ended. Similarly, the conflict contributed to the development of organized labor, which became less militant and more firmly entrenched in the industrial marketplace, and thus more empowered in regular bargaining over wages and working conditions. The nation's largest farmers also realized a political power they had never known before.

The war effected a permanent demographic shift. The migrations toward war production centers reshaped the nation's geographic balance. Cities in the West and the South received a boost that spurred their development. And the baby boom generation born at war's end helps steer the development of all American institutions to this day.

For many groups discriminated against in the past, the war was a vehicle for social and economic gains. Though social reform gave way to other priorities as the United States bowed to what it claimed was military necessity throughout the struggle, women and blacks in particular were able to insist on changes when their own interests coincided with larger military demands. The need for labor, as the draft drew white male workers into the armed forces, opened new opportunities for groups outside the mainstream of American life. The war was a stimulus—and a model—for future change.

The war changed configurations of political power. Americans now looked to the federal government to deal with problems formerly handled in private, or at the state or local level. Decisions to build war plants in certain locations and not others determined

the nature of future industrial development. Housing constructed to meet wartime needs was home to people for years to come. The federal government had played the dominant role in these urban development issues, and even when private initiative rebounded in the 1950s, people still sought guidance and direction from Washington.

The presidency grew even more powerful than it had been in the 1930s. Faced with the most pressing demands any chief executive had ever encountered, Franklin Roosevelt proved willing to experiment and act, just as he had a decade earlier during the Great Depression. His involvement in military and diplomatic affairs, his acceptance of the need to create new agencies to meet mobilization demands, and his willingness to take whatever executive action was necessary to win the war were all factors that contributed to the expansion of the presidential role. Although contractions in the use of executive authority occurred in the postwar years, the basic patterns forged during the war endured.

The war gave a boost to the conservative coalition of southern Democrats and Republicans that had begun to form in the late 1930s. Even as the president assumed more power, Congress demanded a voice and played an influential part in home-front affairs. The New Deal had provided the reform agenda in the 1930s. The conservative coalition in Congress defined what reform efforts were possible in the war and postwar years.

And yet, as John Morton Blum, in *V Was for Victory,* and John W. Jeffries, first in *Testing the Roosevelt Coalition* and later in *Wartime America,* have argued, it would be a serious mistake to see developments of the war period in terms of change alone. Continuity with the past was important, and basic American values survived the conflict intact. As Americans looked ahead, they did so through the lens of the past. They remained attached to the status quo even as they sought to create a more attractive, stable, and secure future.

Jeffries has articulated this argument with the greatest clarity in *Wartime America,* published at the conclusion of the fiftieth anniversary celebrations of World War II. While describing the major changes that took place, he has still observed that "in economic as

in population patterns, the war largely accelerated or confirmed developments long under way." In a variety of different areas, "wartime developments also continued or reinforced prewar trends and patterns, and failed to dispel powerful traditional stereotypes and constraints."

According to this analysis, most Americans, whether in the military or at home, wanted to win the war and then return to the way of life and social patterns they remembered fondly. They hungered for the prosperity they recalled from the 1920s, which once again was possible thanks to the war spending. Their vision of the future included no brave and bold new world, but a revived and refurbished version of the world they had known before. The war restored the self-confidence they had felt prior to the depression and convinced them that what they wanted was within their grasp. The American dream, its contours the same, remained alive and well.

And the changes that unfolded were not always as radical as they seemed at first glance. Many were rooted in trends that had been unfolding for years, even decades, in the United States. Business, for example, had been developing rapidly throughout the post–Civil War period. Wartime changes were simply part of a larger pattern, now even more firmly entrenched. World War II did not forge the military-industrial complex. Many of the same ties and connections existed in the mobilization for World War I.

The list of continuities goes on and on. The process of modern labor organization was rooted in the 1930s, when labor took its greatest steps forward. Wartime migrations, of African Americans and other groups continued a process begun in World War I. Basic political patterns stayed remarkably stable throughout the conflict, with the Roosevelt coalition surviving as the dominant force in electoral life.

Other shifts, the argument for continuity goes, were similarly less dramatic than they initially appeared. Though blacks pressed for reform and sowed the seeds for the postwar civil rights movement, they remained disadvantaged and discriminated against during the war. They were still denied equal access to the armed forces, and even as they took jobs previously denied to them, they had to accept employment restrictions. Women too made signifi-

cant gains, yet they also faced discrimination in their new positions. And even as women improved their economic status, they continued to see themselves—and to be seen by society—in their traditional roles as wives and mothers, roles to which they were pressured to return as soon as the war ended.

Yet even while acknowledging such continuities, the changes that occurred between 1940 and 1945 stand out vividly. Even when seen against a broader perspective, the transformation the United States experienced was profound. Military requirements and production demands resulted in significant social and economic shifts. Responding to the challenges it faced, the United States was undeniably different at the end of the war than it had been at the start. In area after area, the patterns of the postwar period were now in place.

Some of the changes were beneficial; others were not. Some brought benefits to everyone affected; others caused unintended consequences. Business concentration and centralization, for example, made for greater efficiency in the marketplace but posed a threat to both the independent entrepreneur and the ordinary American, who were concerned with personal well-being and advancement in a world where economic mobility was slowly being choked off. Technological and entrepreneurial expertise developed the atomic bomb that helped win the war but in the process created a curse that plagued the world for years to come.

War, by its very nature, has always been a catalyst for change, and World War II was no exception. In democracies and dictatorships alike, enormous shifts took place. In the United States, World War II made Americans more willing to involve themselves— politically and diplomatically—with the outside world. It also expanded their hopes and expectations and forever altered the patterns of their lives at home.

BIBLIOGRAPHICAL ESSAY

For several decades after World War II, historians wrote extensively about the New Deal and the Cold War but neglected the wartime home front in the United States. In the 1970s and 1980s, scholars started to fill that gap with several first-rate comprehensive treatments and a far greater number of specialized studies examining all aspects of the struggle. The first edition of this book was based on those works. In the years since publication of that edition, particularly in the years celebrating the fiftieth anniversary of the war, even more outstanding work has appeared, and this revised edition is informed by that new scholarship.

The best recent book about the war at home is John W. Jeffries, *Wartime America: The World War II Home Front* (Chicago, 1996). It provides a detailed account of all the important issues and an extensive bibliography of recent scholarship. William L. O'Neill, *A Democracy at War: America's Fight at Home and Abroad in World War II* (New York, 1993) offers a good overview of all sides of the struggle. The two best books from the 1970s are Richard Polenberg, *War and Society: The United States, 1941–1945* (Philadelphia, 1972) and John Morton Blum, *V Was for Victory: Politics and American Culture During World War II* (New York, 1976). Polenberg provides an evenhanded and useful assessment of the important wartime developments. Blum includes a fuller sense of the culture and its constraints in his more extended account. Still

helpful to fill out the general picture are Richard R. Lingeman, *Don't You Know There's a War On? The American Home Front, 1941–1945* (New York, 1970), and Geoffrey Perrett, *Days of Sadness, Years of Triumph: The American People, 1939–1945* (New York, 1973). James L. Abrahamson has a very good chapter on World War II in *The American Home Front* (Washington, D.C., 1983). Lee Kennett, *For the Duration: The United States Goes to War, Pearl Harbor—1942* (New York, 1985), examines the first six months of the struggle. Anthologies that can be used to supplement the above works include: Richard Polenberg, ed., *America at War: The Home Front, 1941–1945* (Englewood Cliffs, N.J., 1968); Chester E. Eisinger, ed., *The 1940s: Profile of a Nation in Crisis* (Garden City, N.Y., 1969); and Keith L. Nelson, ed., *The Impact of War on American Life: The Twentieth-Century Experience* (New York, 1971).

On the issue of whether the struggle was a good war, see Studs Terkel, *"The Good War": An Oral History of World War II* (New York, 1984); Paul Fussell, *Wartime: Understanding and Behavior in the Second World War* (New York, 1989); Richard Polenberg, "The Good War? A Reappraisal of How World War II Affected American Society," *The Virginia Magazine of History,* 100 (1992); William L. O'Neill, *A Democracy at War;* and Jeffries, *Wartime America.* On the question of historical memory and its role in reassessing the war, see Edward T. Linenthal and Tom Engelhardt, eds., *History Wars: The* Enola Gay *and Other Battles for the American Past* (New York, 1996).

On Franklin D. Roosevelt, such a dominant figure during the war, there is a vast literature. A number of the standard books about FDR in the early New Deal and war years still give the best sense of the man. To begin, see William E. Leuchtenburg, *Franklin D. Roosevelt and the New Deal, 1932–1940* (New York, 1963); Arthur M. Schlesinger, Jr., *The Age of Roosevelt: The Coming of the New Deal* (Boston, 1958); and *The Age of Roosevelt: The Politics of Upheaval* (Boston, 1960). Equally useful are James MacGregor Burns, *Roosevelt: The Lion and the Fox* (New York, 1956), and *Roosevelt: The Soldier of Freedom* (New York, 1970). The best recent book is Doris Kearns Goodwin, *No Ordinary*

Time: Franklin and Eleanor Roosevelt: The Home Front in World War II (New York, 1994). William E. Leuchtenburg, *In the Shadow of FDR: From Harry Truman to Ronald Reagan,* revised and updated edition (Ithaca, N.Y., 1989) is another useful work. To fill out the picture with speeches and public statements, see Samuel I. Rosenman, ed., *The Public Papers and Addresses of Franklin D. Roosevelt,* X–XIII (New York, 1950).

On war mobilization and economic policy, an official account that provides a good starting point is the United States Bureau of the Budget, *The United States at War: Development and Administration of the War Program by the Federal Government* (Washington, D.C., 1946). John Morton Blum, *From the Morgenthau Diaries: Years of War, 1941–1945* (Boston, 1967) gives a clear overview of events from the vantage point of the secretary of the treasury. Eliot Janeway, *The Struggle for Survival* (New Haven, Conn., 1951) is a still useful description of the governmental effort. Also important is Robert Cuff, "American Mobilization for War, 1917–1945: Political Culture vs. Bureaucratic Administration," in N. F. Dreisziger, ed., *Mobilization for Total War: The Canadian, American and British Experience, 1914–1918, 1939–1945* (Waterloo, Ontario, Canada, 1981). Bartholemew H. Sparrow, *From the Outside In: World War II and the American State* (Princeton, N.J., 1996) examines the larger question of the impact of the war on the nation. Two helpful memoirs are Bruce Catton, *The War Lords of Washington* (New York, 1948), and Donald Nelson, *The Arsenal of Democracy* (New York, 1946). Alan Clive, *State of War: Michigan in World War II* (Ann Arbor, Mich., 1979) gives a full description of the effects of mobilization on one state, while Robert G. Spinney, *World War II in Nashville: Transformation of the Homefront* (Knoxville, Tenn., 1998) provides an assessment of mobilization on one city, and Marc Scott Miller, *The Irony of Victory: World War II and Lowell, Massachusetts* (Urbana, Ill., 1988) describes the impact on another.

For the vindication of John Maynard Keynes and an assessment of war spending on American economic health, see Robert Lekachman, *The Age of Keynes* (New York, 1966). On the growth of government-business ties, the most incisive assessment is Paul

A. C. Koistenen, *The Military-Industrial Complex: A Historical Perspective* (New York, 1980). To study further the consequences of centralization, check the Report of the Smaller War Plants Corporation, *Economic Concentration and World War II* (Washington, D.C., 1946). On the liberal hope that the war could provide a model for peacetime centralization, see Alan Brinkley, *The End of Reform: New Deal Liberalism in Recession and War* (New York, 1995).

There is a full literature on more specific economic questions. Barton J. Bernstein, "The Automobile Industry and the Coming of the Second World War," *Southwestern Social Science Quarterly,* XLVII (1966) examines the conversion to a war footing. On the question of rubber, see William M. Tuttle, Jr., "The Birth of an Industry: The Synthetic Rubber 'Mess' in World War II," *Technology and Culture,* 22 (1981). Stephen B. Adams, *Mr. Kaiser Goes to Washington: The Rise of a Government Entrepreneur* (Chapel Hill, N.C., 1997) is a useful account of Henry Kaiser's role in the war. On tax policy, Randolph E. Paul, *Taxation for Prosperity* (Indianapolis, Ind., 1947) is helpful. John Kenneth Galbraith, "Reflections on Price Control," *Quarterly Journal of Economics,* LX (1949) looks at wartime price questions. For a discussion of the effort to apportion automobile fuel, see James A. Maxwell and Margaret N. Balcom, "Gasoline Rationing in the United States," *Quarterly Journal of Economics,* LX (1946).

There is a growing literature about the atomic bomb. The best account of the development of this new weapon is Richard Rhodes, *The Making of the Atomic Bomb* (New York, 1986). On the question of use of the bomb, see Martin J. Sherwin, *A World Destroyed: The Atomic Bomb and the Grand Alliance* (New York, 1975); Barton J. Bernstein, "Roosevelt, Truman, and the Atomic Bomb, 1941–1945: A Reinterpretation," *Political Science Quarterly,* 90 (1975); J. Samuel Walker, *Prompt and Utter Destruction: Truman and the Use of Atomic Bombs against Japan* (Chapel Hill, N.C., 1997); and Allan M. Winkler, *Life Under a Cloud: American Anxiety about the Atom* (New York, 1993).

For agricultural developments, Walter W. Wilcox, *The Farmer in the Second World War* (Ames, Iowa, 1947) is the place to begin.

A number of good studies document the important role of labor during the war. The best recent treatment is Nelson Lichtenstein, *Labor's War at Home: The CIO in World War II* (New York, 1982). Lichtenstein gives a full sense of labor developments as he describes the increasing bureaucratization of the movement. An earlier but still helpful account is Joel Seidman, *American Labor from Defense to Reconversion* (Chicago, 1953). David Brody, *Workers in Industrial America: Essays on the 20th Century Struggle* (New York, 1980) puts wartime developments into a broader perspective. Irving Bernstein, *Turbulent Years: A History of the American Worker, 1933–1941* (Boston, 1969) provides a vivid view of the background period. Two helpful volumes on the 1940s edited by Colston E. Warne are *Yearbook of American Labor* (New York, 1944), and *Labor in Postwar America* (New York, 1949). On the United Automobile Workers, see Irving Howe and B. J. Widick, *The UAW and Walter Reuther* (New York, 1949) and Martin Glaberman, *Wartime Strikes: The Struggle against the No-Strike Pledge in the UAW* (Detroit, Mich., 1980). On John L. Lewis, see both Saul Alinsky, *John L. Lewis* (New York, 1949), and Melvyn Dubofsky and Warren Van Tine, *John L. Lewis: A Biography* (New York, 1977).

The question of the social impact of World War II can be pursued in a variety of different ways. Lingeman, *Don't You Know There's a War On?*, and Perrett, *Days of Sadness, Years of Triumph* both describe domestic changes and developments, from fads to favorite pastimes. Philip D. Beidler, *The Good War's Greatest Hits: World War II and American Remembering* (Athens, Ga., 1998) provides an overview of popular culture. Blum, in *V Was for Victory,* gives a good sense of the wartime mood in once-again prosperous times. Tom Brokaw, *The Greatest Generation* (New York, 1998) describes the lives of a variety of Americans at home and abroad during the struggle. Richard White shows the effect of the war on the West in *"It's Your Misfortune and None of My Own": A New History of the American West* (Norman, Okla., 1991). Clive, *State of War,* gives a real feeling for the impact of war on the people of Michigan. William M. Tuttle, Jr., shows the effects of the war on children in *"Daddy's Gone to War": The Sec-*

ond World War in the Lives of America's Children (New York, 1993). On the issue of gays during the war, see John D'Emilio, *Sexual Politics, Sexual Communities: The Making of a Homosexual Minority in the United States, 1940–1970* (Chicago, 1983) and Allan Bérubé, *Coming Out under Fire: The History of Gay Men and Women in World War II* (New York, 1990). Two older treatments that remain useful are Francis E. Merrill, *Social Problems on the Home Front* (New York, 1948), and William F. Ogburn, ed., *American Society in Wartime* (Chicago, 1943). For a perceptive collection of essays that tells veterans about the changes that occurred in the United States, see Jack Goodman, ed., *While You Were Gone* (New York, 1946).

On the soldiers' war, see D. Clayton James and Anne Sharp Wells, *From Pearl Harbor to V-J Day: The American Armed Forces in World War II* (Chicago, 1995); Lee Kennett, *G.I.: The American Soldier in World War II* (New York, 1987); and John Ellis, *The Sharp End: The Fighting Man in World War II* (New York, 1980). See too Fussell, *Wartime,* as well as the dispatches of Ernie Pyle in David Nichols, ed., *Ernie's War: The Best of Ernie Pyle's World War II Dispatches* (New York, 1986). Stephen Speilberg's film *Saving Private Ryan* (1998) vividly captures the experience of World War II combat.

On more specific social issues, the literature is growing. To pursue the question of war aims, at both public and policy levels, see Blum, *V Was for Victory* and Allan M. Winkler, *The Politics of Propaganda: The Office of War Information, 1942–1945* (New Haven, Conn., 1978). For population shifts, Henry S. Shryock, Jr., and Hope T. Eldridge, "Internal Migration in Peace and War," *American Sociological Review,* XII (1947) is useful. Even more helpful on the migrations and the consequences for public policy is Philip J. Funigiello, *The Challenge to Urban Liberalism:Federal-City Relations during World War II* (Knoxville, Tenn., 1978).

Other kinds of works also help to describe American society in the war. Harriette Arnow's moving novel *The Dollmaker* (New York, 1954) vividly conveys the crowded conditions and human difficulties in wartime Detroit. Pictures can be equally important. Ronald H. Bailey and the editors of Time-Life Books have done a first-rate job of collecting photographs in *The Home Front:*

U.S.A. (Alexandria, Va., 1977). William L. Bird, Jr., and Harry Rubenstein, *Design for Victory: World War II Posters on the American Home Front* (New York, 1998) is an outstanding collection of wartime posters. Stan Cohen, *V for Victory: America's Home Front during World War II* (Missoula, Mont., 1991) is another good compilation of wartime images. Oral history, likewise, can give a feeling for the period, and Terkel, *"The Good War"* and Mark Jonathon Harris, Franklin D. Mitchell, and Steven J. Schechter, *The Homefront: America during World War II* (New York, 1984) are especially useful.

On film, see Bernard F. Dick, *The Star-Spangled Screen: The American World War II Film* (Lexington, Ky., 1985); Clayton R. Koppes and Gregory D. Black, *Hollywood Goes to War: How Politics, Profits and Propaganda Shaped World War II Movies* (Berkeley and Los Angeles, Ca., 1987); and John Whiteclay Chambers II, and David Culbert, *World War II, Film, and History* (New York, 1996).

In recent years, there has been a good deal of creative work done on the status of women in World War II. The best starting point is William Chafe, *The American Woman: Her Changing Social, Economic, and Political Roles, 1920–1970* (New York, 1972). Since Chafe wrote, a number of other scholars have examined in greater detail shifting work patterns and the related question of social role. Two very useful surveys of women's wartime experience are: Karen Anderson, *Wartime Women: Sex Roles, Family Relations, and the Status of Women during World War II* (Westport, Conn., 1981), and Susan M. Hartmann, *The Home Front and Beyond: American Women in the 1940s* (Boston, 1982). Similarly helpful are two studies by Eleanor Straub, "United States Government Policy toward Civilian Women during World War II," *Prologue,* 5 (1973), and "Government Policy toward Civilian Women during World War II," (Ph.D. dissertation, Emory University, 1973), as well as a perceptive study by D'Ann Campbell, *Women at War with America: Private Lives in a Patriotic Era* (Cambridge, Mass., 1985). Elaine Tyler May, *Homeward Bound: American Families in the Cold War Era* (New York, 1988) has a good chapter on the war years. See also Leila Rupp's thoughtful comparative treatment, *Mobilizing Women for War:*

German and American Propaganda, 1939–1945 (Princeton, N.J., 1978). For women's own voices, see Judy Barrett Litoff and David C. Smith, eds., *Since You Went Away: World War II Letters from American Women on the Home Front* (Lawrence, Kans., 1991) and *American Women in a World at War: Contemporary Accounts from World War II* (Wilmington, Del., 1997).

On more specific topics, there are a number of pertinent works. For women's military role, begin with the official history, Mattie E. Treadwell, *The United States Army in World War II: Volume VIII: The Women's Army Corps* (Washington, D.C., 1954) and then see Paula Nassen Poulos, ed., *A Women's War Too: U.S. Women in the Military in World War II* (Washington, D.C., 1996).

On women's employment, see Sherna Berger Gluck, *Rosie the Riveter Revisited: Women, the War, and Social Change* (Boston, 1987) and Maureen Honey, *Creating Rosie the Riveter: Class, Gender and Propaganda during World War II* (Amherst, Mass., 1984). A still useful early book is Constance McLaughlin Green, *The Role of Women as Production Workers in War Plants in the Connecticut Valley* (Northampton, Mass., 1948). Alan Clive, "Women Workers in World War II: Michigan as a Test Case," *Labor History,* 20 (1979) is also helpful, as is Antonette Chambers Noble, "Utah's Rosies: Women in the Utah War Industries during World War II, *Utah Historical Quarterly* 59 (1991). On the same subject, see as well Marc Miller, "Working Women and World War II," *New England Quarterly,* 53 (1980); Karen Beck Skold, "The Job He Left Behind: American Women in the Shipyards during World War II," in Carol R. Berkin and Clara M. Lovett, eds., *Women, War and Revolution* (New York, 1980); and Paddy Quick, "Rosie the Riveter: Myths and Realities," *Radical America,* 9 (1975).

Three broader treatments that provide perspective about women during the war are Alice Kessler-Harris, *Out to Work: A History of Wage-Earning Women in the United States* (New York, 1982); Carl N. Degler, *At Odds: Women and the Family in America From the Revolution to the Present* (New York, 1980); and Peter Gabriel Filene, *Him/Her/Self: Sex Roles in Modern America* (New York, 1974).

The role of African Americans during World War II has also received a good deal of attention. Neil A. Wynn, *The Afro-American and the Second World War* (New York, 1976) provides a comprehensive overview and is the place to start. Richard M. Dalfiume's article, "The Forgotten Years of the Negro Revolution," *Journal of American History*, 55 (1968) is still essential, and his book, *Desegregation of the United States Armed Forces: Fighting on Two Fronts, 1939–1953* (Columbia, Mo., 1969) is important on the military question. Another important book on the military aspect is Ulysses Lee, *The Employment of Negro Troops* (Washington, D.C., 1966). Other useful studies include: Lee Finkle, *Forum for Protest: The Black Press During World War II* (Rutherford, N.J., 1975); John Kirby, *Black Americans in the Roosevelt Era: Liberalism and Race* (Knoxville, Tenn., 1980); and August Meier and Elliott Rudwick, *CORE: A Study in the Civil Rights Movement, 1942–1968* (New York, 1973). For a more contemporary view, see Rayford W. Logan, ed., *What the Negro Wants* (Chapel Hill, N.C., 1944), and Robert Weaver, *Negro Labor* (New York, 1946). See too the chapter on the war in John Hope Franklin and Alfred A. Moss, Jr., *From Slavery to Freedom: A History of African Americans*, 7th ed. (New York, 1994).

On the impact of the war on black women, see Jacqueline Jones, *Labor of Love, Labor of Sorrow: Black Women, Work, and the Family, from Slavery to the Present* (New York, 1985).

For the difficulties of the Fair Employment Practices Committee, the best recent works are Merl E. Reed, *Seedtime for the Modern Civil Rights Movement: The President's Committee on Fair Employment Practice, 1941–1946* (Baton Rouge, La., 1991) and Andrew E. Kersten, *Race, Jobs, and the War: The FEPC in the Midwest, 1941–1946* (Urbana, Ill., 2000). Other helpful works are: Louis Ruchames, *Race, Jobs and Politics: The Story of FEPC* (Chapel Hill, N.C., 1948); Louis C. Kesselman, *The Social Politics of FEPC* (Chapel Hill, N.C., 1948); Will Maslow, "FEPC—A Case History in Parliamentary Maneuver," *University of Chicago Law Review*, XIII (1946); and Allan M. Winkler, "The Philadelphia Transit Strike of 1944," *Journal of American History*, LIX (1972).

Wartime racial violence has come under close scrutiny. Works on the riot in Detroit include: Robert Shogan and Tom Craig, *The Detroit Race Riot: A Study in Violence* (Philadelphia, 1964); Alfred McClung Lee and Norman D. Humphrey, *Race Riot* (New York, 1943); and Harvard Sitkoff, "The Detroit Race Riot of 1943," *Michigan History,* LIII (1969). For a treatment of the Harlem uprising, see Dominic J. Capeci, *The Harlem Riot of 1943* (Philadelphia, 1977).

A number of biographical and autobiographical treatments of major black figures give a fuller sense of the struggle for civil rights. See in particular Jervis Anderson, *A. Philip Randolph: A Biographical Portrait* (New York, 1973), and Walter White, *A Rising Wind* (Garden City, N.Y., 1945).

The literature on Latinos is less voluminous. Rodolfo Acuña, *Occupied America: A History of Chicanos,* 3rd ed. (New York, 1988) is helpful, as is Ronald Takaki, *A Different Mirror: A History of Multicultural America* (Boston, 1993). See too George J. Sánchez, *Becoming Mexican American: Ethnicity, Culture, and Identity in Chicano Los Angeles, 1900–1945* (New York, 1993). Other works include: Robert C. Jones, *Mexican War Workers in the United States* (Washington, D.C., 1945); Carey McWilliams, *North from Mexico: The Spanish Speaking People of the United States* (Philadelphia, 1949), and Stanley Steiner, *La Raza: The Mexican Americans* (New York, 1970).

On American Indians in the war, the literature is similarly sparse. The best book is Alison R. Bernstein, *American Indians and World War II: Toward a New Era in Indian Affairs* (Norman, Okla., 1991). Peter Iverson, *"We Are Still Here": American Indians in the Twentieth Century* (Wheeling, Ill., 1998) is useful on the war years. John Collier, "The Indian in a Wartime Nation," *The Annals of the American Academy of Political and Social Science,* 223 (1942) is a contemporary assessment. Alvin M. Josephy, Jr., *Now That the Buffalo's Gone: A Study of Today's Indians* (New York, 1982) describes in detail Indian struggles over the past several decades and provides a useful perspective.

For the Italian-American experience, see John P. Diggins, *Mussolini and Fascism: The View from America* (Princeton, N.J.,

1972); Rudolf J. Vecoli, "The Coming of Age of the Italian Americans, 1945-1974," *Ethnicity,* 5 (1978); and Lawrence F. Pisani, *The Italian in America: A Social Study and History* (New York, 1957). Blum, *V Was for Victory,* has a useful section on wartime difficulties.

There has been a more searching examination of the Japanese-American experience during the war. Roger Daniels provides the best starting point in *Concentration Camps U.S.A.: Japanese Americans and World War II* (New York, 1971), *The Decision to Relocate the Japanese Americans* (Philadelphia, 1975), and *Prisoners Without Trial: Japanese Americans in World War II* (New York, 1993). John Armor and Peter Wright, *Manzanar* (New York, 1988) contains photographs by Ansel Adams and a commentary by John Hersey. Other useful accounts include: Page Smith, *Democracy on Trial: The Japanese American Evacuation and Relocation in World War II* (New York, 1995); Thomas James, *Exile Within: The Schooling of Japanese Americans, 1942–1945* (Cambridge, Mass., 1987); Mike Masaoka with Bill Hosokawa, *They Call Me Moses Masaoka: An American Saga* (New York, 1987); Morton Grodzins, *Americans Betrayed: Politics and the Japanese Evacuation* (Chicago, 1949); Jacobus ten Broek, Edward N. Barnhart, and Floyd W. Matson, *Prejudice, War and the Constitution* (Berkeley, California, 1954); and Audrie Girdner and Anne Loftis, *The Great Betrayal* (London, 1969). See too Bill Hosokawa, *Nisei: The Quiet Americans* (New York, 1969), and Michi Weglyn, *Years of Infamy: The Untold Story of America's Concentration Camps* (New York, 1976). For the court cases, Peter Irons, *Justice At War* (New York, 1983) is the best source.

On the Jewish experience in World War II, see Henry L. Feingold, *The Politics of Rescue: The Roosevelt Administration and the Holocaust, 1938–1945* (New Brunswick, N.J., 1970) and David S. Wyman, *Paper Walls: America and the Refugee Crisis, 1938–1941* (Amherst, Mass., 1968) and *The Abandonment of the Jews: America and the Holocaust, 1941–1945* (New York, 1984).

There is a good deal of literature on the politics of the Second World War. John W. Jeffries, *Testing the Roosevelt Coalition: Connecticut Society and Politics in the Era of World War II* (Knoxville,

Tenn., 1979) is an outstanding state study that goes beyond the Connecticut borders to give a full sense of the political issues of the war. In *Wartime America,* Jeffries amplifies on many of these themes. On the Roosevelt coalition itself, see Samuel Lubell, *The Future of American Politics* (New York, 1951). For the growing opposition to Roosevelt that culminated in the formation of a conservative coalition, see James T. Patterson, *Congressional Conservatism and the New Deal: The Growth of the Conservative Coalition in Congress, 1933–1939* (Lexington, Ky., 1967).

For the impact of that coalition in Congress, Roland Young, *Congressional Politics in the Second World War* (New York, 1956) is still helpful. Even more pertinent and substantive is Richard N. Chapman, *Contours of Public Policy, 1939–1945* (New York, 1981). See also John Robert Moore, "The Conservative Coalition in the United States Senate, 1942–1945," *Journal of Southern History,* XXXIII (1967), and Donald R. McCoy, "Republican Opposition in Wartime, 1941–1945," *Mid-America,* XLIX (1967). John A. Salmond, *The Civilian Conservation Corps, 1933–1942* (Durham, N.C., 1967) describes the fate of one New Deal agency during the war.

For Roosevelt's efforts in connection with the G.I. Bill, Keith Olson, *The G.I. Bill, the Veterans, and the Colleges* (Lexington, Ky., 1974), and David R. B. Ross, *Preparing for Ulysses, 1940–1946* (New York, 1969) are both useful.

Studies focusing on important individuals provide a fuller sense of political dynamics. On the Republican side, a number of the more helpful ones include: Joseph Barnes, *Willkie* (New York, 1952); Donald Bruce Johnson, *The Republican Party and Wendell Willkie* (Urbana, Ill., 1960); Barry Keith Beyer, "Thomas E. Dewey, 1933–1947," (Ph.D. dissertation, University of Rochester, 1962); and James T. Patterson, *Mr. Republican: A Biography of Robert A. Taft* (Boston, 1972). Similar works relating to Democrats are Russell Lord, *The Wallaces of Iowa* (Boston, 1947); Norman Markowitz, *The Rise and Fall of the People's Century: Henry A. Wallace and American Liberalism, 1941–1948* (New York; 1973); John Morton Blum, ed., *The Price of Vision: The Diary of Henry A. Wallace, 1942–1946* (Boston, 1973); and Robert

E. Sherwood, *Roosevelt and Hopkins* (New York, 1948). On Roosevelt himself in political campaigns, Burns, *Roosevelt: The Soldier of Freedom* contains a good deal of pertinent material. For Truman, see Alonzo Hamby, *Man of the People: A Life of Harry S. Truman* (New York, 1995) and David McCullough, *Truman* (New York, 1992) to begin further examination.

On the question of the growth of presidential power, Richard Polenberg, *Reorganizing Roosevelt's Government: The Controversy over Executive Reorganization, 1936–1939* (Cambridge, Mass., 1966) provides necessary background on the question of the establishment of the Executive Office. Arthur M. Schlesinger, Jr., *The Imperial Presidency* (Boston, 1973) is the essential treatment of the expansion of executive authority, both during the war and at other times.

To pursue more fully the debate over change versus continuity during World War II, begin with Jeffries, *Wartime America*. See too the introduction in Clive, *State of War* and the last chapter in Jeffries, *Testing the Roosevelt Coalition*. Among the scholars who have documented substantial change are Polenberg, in *War and Society*; Perrett, in *Days of Sadness, Years of Triumph;* and Burns, in *Roosevelt: The Soldier of Freedom*. John Morton Blum observes the important continuities in *V Was for Victory,* as does Jeffries in both of his books.

INDEX

DATE DUE